Jan Brook 64422   U3
2.11.89   6·95

C000090882

EDUCATION, CULTURE AND THE NATIONAL CURRICULUM

EDUCATION, CULTURE AND THE NATIONAL CURRICULUM

DENIS LAWTON

Professor of Education and Director
University of London Institute of Education

HODDER AND STOUGHTON
LONDON   SYDNEY   AUCKLAND   TORONTO

Copyright © 1989 Denis Lawton

First published 1989

British Library Cataloguing in Publication Data

Lawton, Denis, *1931-*
    Education, culture and the National Curriculum
    1. Great Britain. Schools. Curriculum
    I. Title
    375′.00941

    ISBN 0-340-50509-5

All rights reserved. No part of this publication may be reproduced or transmitted in any form or by any means, electronically or mechanically, including photocopying, recording or any information storage or retrieval system, without either the prior permission in writing from the publisher or a licence, permitting restricted copying, issued by the Copyright Licensing Agency, 33-34 Alfred Place, London, WC1E 7DP.

Typeset in Linotron Ehrhardt by Taurus Graphics, Abingdon.
Printed and bound in Great Britain for
Hodder and Stoughton Educational,
a division of Hodder and Stoughton Ltd,
Mill Road, Dunton Green, Sevenoaks, Kent
by J. W. Arrowsmith Ltd, Bristol BS3 2NT.

CONTENTS

ACKNOWLEDGMENTS

Since this book is partly a rewritten version of earlier texts, it would be impossible to thank everyone, individually, who has commented on my views and suggested alternatives. I am grateful to all of them. However, I would like to mention specifically those who have contributed directly to this book: Dr Michael Kingdon who allowed me to read some of his writings, published and unpublished, about examinations and assessment, and who made detailed comments on Chapter 8; Professor Peter Gordon and Clyde Chitty who read the whole manuscript in draft form; Joyce Broomhall who helped to eliminate errors as well as producing the final version of the Bibliography; and my wife Joan who prepared each draft and the final typescript with only occasional signs of irritation.

PREFACE

One of the problems of curriculum studies is that it is subject to frequent change. The school curriculum in any society has to adjust to other kinds of social change as well as to disciplines which impinge on the intellectual study of curriculum planning. This book is a reflection of those adjustments: it is intended to replace *Curriculum Studies and Educational Planning* (1983) which was itself written as an acknowledgment that *Social Change, Educational Theory and Curriculum Planning* (1973) was out of date in many respects by the early 1980s.

I have preserved some sections of *Curriculum Studies and Educational Planning* but rather than simply attempting to up-date the book in the light of the events of the last five years, I thought it preferable to rethink several theoretical issues as well as to discuss the relevant education and political events which had taken place since 1983. The Education Act 1988 has correctly been described as the most significant legislation for education since 1944, and much will be written about the Act in its own right. However, the national curriculum as formulated in the Act needs to be seen in the context of theories of education and theories of social change.

Like *Curriculum Studies and Educational Planning*, this book will also employ a process of cultural analysis as a basis for curriculum planning. Thus, curriculum is defined as a selection from the culture of a society. Such a definition is uncontroversial (what else could a curriculum be?) – but controversy may begin when details of this selection from the culture emerge. Before that point can be reached, the culture has to be analysed, classified and 'matched' against existing curricula. At this stage inadequacies and contradictions can be perceived, and improvements suggested. However, the process of curriculum planning or replanning is not an automatic matching exercise: values are always involved. Whilst it may not be possible to reconcile differences in educational views within a society, it is important at least to attempt to clarify the issues and values prior to implementing a plan.

Denis Lawton 1988

1 CURRICULUM STUDIES AND CURRICULUM PLANNING

Curriculum Studies is still a relatively new subject in the UK and to describe oneself as a Professor of Curriculum Studies may provoke raised eyebrows or demands for explanation. The curriculum is often taken for granted rather than studied, and discussions of curriculum tend to centre on minor adjustments to traditional timetables rather than fundamental rethinking of aims and purposes. One of the criticisms of the Kenneth Baker proposals for a national curriculum, 1987–88, was that it only tinkered with existing subjects when what was required was a more fundamental re-examination of what young people in the 1980s need by way of knowledge, skills and experience.

Curriculum studies in the UK began to be regarded as a serious area for intellectual enquiry in the 1960s, when curriculum development was already taking place pragmatically in the form of Nuffield Science and Mathematics projects. These curriculum projects provoked questions and stimulated the study of curriculum in a number of ways and at a number of different levels. In the process of changing the existing science curriculum, for example, those advocating change were forced to answer such questions as

'Why teach science?'
'Should all children learn science?'
'What kind of science?'
'What is science?'
'What is school science?' and so on.

In some respects curriculum studies involved much of what already existed as general educational theory, but with more direct reference to teaching and learning in classrooms. The subject as a kind of academic discipline was further stimulated by the creation of the Schools Council in 1964 which not only provided funding for many more curriculum projects, but also encouraged, indirectly, some questions about the traditional curriculum and its adequacy.

In the USA curriculum studies had started earlier, both as an intellectual discipline and as a practical activity designed to improve the quality of learning. There is a tradition stretching from at least as far back as Bobbitt (1918), who wanted to reduce curriculum planning to specifying a few thousand highly specific tasks, to Tyler (1949), whose rationale laid the basis for much later discussion (see Chapter 2). Unfortunately, Tyler's rationale was frequently misunderstood and transformed into a very rigid behaviouristic model based on specific behavioural objectives. The misapplication of Tyler has occasionally floated across the

Atlantic, but the cultural resistance to that and other kinds of planning is very strong.

Curriculum planning is not an activity which came easily to the English educators. Planning involves putting into operation a theory of some kind, but the English tend to be practical, common-sense individuals who view theories and ideas with great caution. The weakness of this common-sense, amateur approach is, however, that it leaves teachers vulnerable to attack from outside the profession: if teachers cannot convincingly explain why they have adopted new mathematics or a modular curriculum then parents and others may feel entitled to criticise them. This attack may take the form of raising questions about 'standards' because that is usually the easiest way of denouncing innovation. In future years it will be essential for teachers to be able to justify their curricular decisions and classroom practices; if they attempt to do this in a completely non-theoretical way, they are likely to find themselves in difficulties.

The history of the Schools Council provides an excellent illustration of the British dislike of theory. The Schools Council will probably be remembered for funding a large number of interesting projects based on traditional subjects or attempting to develop aspects of an interdisciplinary curriculum; the Council never succeeded in outlining a systematic approach to the whole curriculum. Two attempts were made to discuss the whole curriculum but without real success. The first was in 1975 when after many discussions and several attempts to produce an agreed document, a very bland Working Paper eventually appeared *(The Whole Curriculum 13–16)*. This failure was partly the result of a policy which had developed among the teacher unions of resisting anything which could be seen as a centrally planned uniform curriculum. For the National Union of Teachers (NUT), National Association of Schoolmasters and Union of Women Teachers (NASUWT) and others, planning the curriculum was the responsibility of individual schools and teachers; Schools Council projects should offer packages of materials from which teachers could choose in order to build up their own curriculum.

The second attempt to produce a plan for the whole curriculum was made towards the end of the existence of the Schools Council. By then (1980–81) it was clear that one of the criticisms of the Council was that it lacked a coherent view of the curriculum as a whole, and a Working Party was somewhat reluctantly set up. It was a classic case of too little, too late: instead of commissioning a major study, the Schools Council Working Party, after a few meetings, produced *The Practical Curriculum* (1981). The document lacked any adequate theoretical underpinning and had very little impact on schools or projects.

One explanation for these failures has already been given – the hostility of teacher unions – but a more fundamental reason was the disinclination of teachers to engage in any discussion of the curriculum in theoretical terms. Good teachers regarded themselves as practical people who had no need of curriculum theory – the title of the Schools Council document, *The Practical Curriculum* was meant to appeal to classroom practitioners rather than to educational theorists.

Such rejection of theory was a costly mistake but, on the other hand, teachers in

England were right to reject some kinds of curriculum theory. They were right to be suspicious of those approaches to curriculum planning which begin with theory, and then proceed, step by step, to put some kind of *system* into practice. Teachers know intuitively that this is not what happens in the real world. Today it may be sensible to base a plan for building a new bridge on theoretical principles derived from mathematics and physics, but we should also remember that bridges were built long before engineers and physicists outlined their theories. In other words, in practical activities such as engineering, education and medicine, practice tends to precede theory; but this does not mean that theory is unnecessary – at a later stage theory refines practice and it eventually becomes difficult to improve practice without theoretical analysis.

When a politician or an employer criticises a school curriculum because it allegedly does not turn out young people ready for the world of work, there is a theory behind that apparently common-sense view: namely that one of the purposes of education is to prepare the young for working life. Few would suggest that this is the only purpose of education, so in order to discuss the subject sensibly, it becomes necessary to identify the other purposes of education in an advanced industrial society, and even to begin to make judgements about their relative importance. This is the beginning of the process of cultural analysis which will be employed in this book. (See Chapter 3).

Unfortunately, arguments about education or the curriculum are rarely conducted in a completely rational, analytical way: assertions of values or priorities provoke counter-assertions without reference to any means of judging what might be regarded as more appropriate or even superior. Every statement that a teacher makes in a classroom is value-laden, connected with ideas about the purpose of education, probably connected with the more general values and beliefs, and maybe with the purpose of life. So it is for educational planners and curriculum developers, whether they realise it or not. An assumption of this book is that it is important for teachers and planners to be aware of their values and to be able to make them explicit.

Some curriculum developers in the 1950s who were concerned with revising science curricula, claimed to be 'value-free'. However, they soon had to face questions about the purpose of school science: was the aim to provide enough scientists for industry? Or was the purpose of school science to equip all young people with an understanding of a very significant aspect of their social and physical environment? It is impossible to answer those kinds of questions without engaging in discussions of values.

Teachers and educational administrators, as well as politicians, operate with some kind of 'social theory' in the sense of sets of assumptions, values and ideas about a good society. These views may lack coherence, and some assumptions may contradict others. One purpose of curriculum studies is to clarify such issues and questions, to relate isolated points of view to more general ideologies, and to make clear what the theoretical and practical choices are. Curriculum studies is, therefore, concerned with theories rather than with a theory. In this sense curriculum studies may have some similarity to studying politics. It would be wrong for a university course in political science to conclude by telling the students how to vote at the next election. It would be equally inappropriate for a book on curriculum studies to specify exactly what a curriculum should include; but in both cases the choices should be clearer and the basis of decision making more rational as a result of a course of study undertaken.

In pluralistic societies like ours, individuals agree about many important values and beliefs, but disagree about others. For some purposes of analysis, it may be useful to classify individuals according to their belief systems. In politics we use terms like 'conservative', 'liberal', 'social democrat'; in education it has been suggested that there are at least three basic educational ideologies (Skilbeck, 1976) each of which generates a different type of curriculum theory:

1   Classical humanism
2   Progressivism
3   Reconstructionism

These ideologies are 'ideal types' in the sense that they may not exist in a pure form – individual teachers could easily find themselves in at least two of the categories – but some aspects of one ideology may be incompatible with beliefs from one of the others.

CLASSICAL HUMANISM

Classical humanism as an educational ideology can be traced back to Greece in the 4th century BC when Plato developed the idea of cultural heritage, whose custodians were a class of 'guardians'. The ideology survived the Middle Ages and the Renaissance, and was the basis of Matthew Arnold's (1869) view of education. T.S. Eliot (1948) continued the tradition. An essential feature of classical humanism is that it associates traditional culture and values with a small 'elite'. The elite, referred to by Plato as 'men of gold', were to receive an education quite different from the other two groups – 'men of silver' and 'men of bronze'.

The classical humanist curriculum concentrates on cultural heritage; those kinds of knowledge worked out over centuries to give the best in terms of literature, music, and history. For some, science is a recent but important addition. In the UK the development of the classical humanist curriculum can be traced through the medieval trivium and quadrivium to the idea of the renaissance man, to the nineteenth-century public school and Christian gentlemen educated at Oxford or Cambridge.

There are those who continue to advocate classical humanism as the model for real education today but, in most democratic societies, education is now regarded as a 'good end' in its own right which ought to be available to all rather than being the privilege of a small elite. It is also an incomplete view of education since it concerns itself with only one kind of intellectual experience, whereas twentieth-century society makes many more demands on future citizens. The kind of classical humanist subject-matter which served admirably as 'a badge of rank' for nineteenth-century gentlemen cannot easily be transformed into the kind of educational programme suitable for the majority in the 1990s. Nevertheless, anyone who cares to examine the educational arguments of the 1970s, for example, in the *Black Papers* (Cox and Dyson, 1969) will find clear examples of classical humanism.

PROGRESSIVISM

This ideology also has a long history: its most famous text is Jean-Jacques Rousseau's *Emile* (1762). Whereas classical humanism is knowledge-centred, progressivism is openly child-centred, representing a romantic rejection of traditional values and practices. The transmission of cultural heritage is abandoned in favour of the goal of the child discovering for himself and following his own impulses. Childhood becomes important in its own right and is no longer regarded as preparation for adulthood; freedom is more important than social order.

Progressivism was made into a specific educational programme by other writers such as Pestalozzi and Froebel. One much publicised twentieth-century progressivist was A.S. Neill. Elements of the ideology were also apparent in the Plowden Report (1963) *Children and Their Primary Schools*. Many progressivists would reject the idea of a planned curriculum altogether; if there were a curriculum it would be based on experiences and topics chosen by the pupils themselves, and 'discovery' would be the dominant form of pedagogy. Knowledge of facts would be of little importance, although acquisition of concepts and generalisations might be an aim. Children's own writing and painting would be seen as of greater value than appreciating the achievements of others. In its most extreme form romantic individualism would reject traditional knowledge and values completely, in favour of the young discovering their own way of life; others, including Rousseau, seemed to want to manipulate the young into 'discovering' desirable solutions.

The main objection to progressivism is that it is based on an over-optimistic view of human nature. A. S. Neill and others have assumed that human beings are naturally good but become corrupted by an evil society. The evidence is against this ideology: children possess an innate selfishness which is only made tolerable by the influence of adults insisting on social conventions; a child only becomes truly human by developing socially as well as individually. Children and societies are complex mixtures of good and evil, and education consists ideally of encouraging the good and eliminating the evil. However, child-centred ideology was to some extent a healthy reaction against the inhuman treatment of children witnessed by Rousseau in the eighteenth century and indeed by A. S. Neill in the twentieth century. Moreover, the developmental approach advocated by Rousseau has been refined by Piaget and others into a scientific approach to children's learning. Not all of progressivism can be rejected as romantic child-centred sentimentality; but as a complete view of education and curriculum it is deeply flawed.

RECONSTRUCTIONISM

If classical humanism is knowledge-centred, and progressivism is child-centred, reconstructionism might be described as society-centred. However, this would be an over-simplification since an important part of reconstructionism is to see individuals and society as harmoniously integrated rather than in opposition. It might be more helpful to regard the three ideologies in Hegelian terms of thesis, antithesis and synthesis: classical humanism being the original traditional 'thesis', progressivism providing a radical reaction against classical humanism, with reconstructionism emerging as a synthesis of both, preserving the best but developing a new ideology differing from the two that preceded it.

Social reconstructionists see education as a way of improving society, and at the same time developing individual members of society. In the USA reconstructionism is often associated with John Dewey (although Tanner and Tanner (1980) make a distinction between Dewey's 'experimentalism' and 'social reconstructionism' which was a more radical ideology). Dewey saw the experimental methods of science as an appropriate approach to social questions. For Dewey, democracy was not simply a form of government but a way of life which provided maximum opportunities for individual growth. Education for all was a desirable aspect of a democratic society as well as a means of achieving a better democracy. Education provided opportunities for individual growth, thus ensuring an improving quality of life for individuals as well as improving the quality of society itself.

The reconstructionist curriculum lays stress upon social values: experiences appropriate for developing citizenship and social cooperation. Knowledge is by no means ignored, but knowledge for its own sake is questionable. Knowledge is justified in terms of social needs, not in terms of custom, nor cultural heritage *per se*. Subjects will not be taken for granted, and various patterns of 'integrated studies' may tend to assume more importance than subject compartments. Science and mathematics will be taught to all pupils, not only because they are useful for vocational preparation, but because they are important for an understanding of the society and the physical environment.

The view taken in the following chapters is a democratic, non-utopian version of social reconstructionism. This is not to imply that there is no value in the other two ideologies but that, given a democratic society which values certain kinds of freedom, a version of social reconstructionism is the most appropriate planning model. Progressivism and classical humanism will be seen not to stand up to an analysis of the needs of individuals growing up in an industrial society in the last part of the twentieth century. To use reconstructionism as a basis of curriculum planning is, however, only the first stage in deciding on a curriculum, as we shall see in the chapters that follow, and this commitment does not answer all the questions which will arise about curriculum content.

It is not, of course, the case that the three ideologies outlined above are the only ones possible. Skilbeck, for example, refers to a bureaucratic-technicist ideology which has some links with utilitarianism; but there is a good deal of agreement in the UK, USA and Australia on the definition of three basic educational ideologies, despite some confusing differences in terminology. Tanner and Tanner (1980), for example, postulate three basic 'philosophies', the conservative, the progressivist and the romantic, each of which can be sub-divided: some conservatives (Skilbeck's classical humanists) may advocate a 'great books of the past' approach to curriculum (the perennialists); other conservatives, of a somewhat less reactionary disposition, would base the curriculum on traditional forms of knowledge or subject disciplines (the essentialists). Tanner and Tanner's progressivists are not the same as Skilbeck's progressivists but are closer to his reconstructionists; but this group is sub-divided by Tanner and Tanner into experimentalism, the most notable exponent of which was Dewey, and social reconstructionists who would be more radical, advocating using education to question and even reject some aspects of current social values. Finally, Tanner and Tanner's romantics would include those referred to by Skilbeck as progressivists as well as a separate group of existentialists.

It is also important not to ignore the relation between educational ideologies and deep-rooted social and political beliefs as well as psychological attitudes. Classical humanists, for example, tend to be associated with political conservativism. Other writers have pointed out the existence of fundamental differences in beliefs about human nature which affect social and educational views. Many would agree with Hobbes (1588–1679) that human beings are essentially selfish; they would reject not only progressivist ideology but probably any child-centred practices in education.

On the other hand, the above educational ideologies cannot be simply equated with political ideologies concerned with the control of and access to educational opportunity. There will be some overlap but not total convergence. Later in this book I shall be discussing four ideological positions concerning the debate between those who would plan education and those who would leave education to market forces. In Chapter 6 I identify four positions on the ideological spectrum – the privatisers, the minimalists, the pluralists and the comprehensive planners. Those who favour planning will tend to support greater state provision and expenditure at all levels of education, whereas the advocates of the market want to minimise public expenditure and encourage parents and others to spend their own money on education and training if they see this as a benefit. There is a danger of this dispute in education developing into a false opposition between justice and freedom. The ideological differences are, however, much more complex, as Rawls (1972), Dworkin (1977) and Ackerman (1980) have shown. At times of economic

7

recession, however, it is easy for social justice in education to become a lower priority. This has happened in many part of the world, including the USA, Australia and New Zealand since the economic problems associated with oil prices began in the 1970s. There is a temptation in those societies to retreat to more elitist, less egalitarian policies with an emphasis on vocational training rather than education for the majority.

SUMMARY

Education cannot be value-free. Different value systems or ideologies will generate different curricula. In twentieth-century democratic societies attempts are being made to educate all young people instead of focusing on the elite minority favoured by classical humanism. Progressivism is likewise rejected, partly because its view of human nature is unrealistically optimistic, and partly because it fails to relate curriculum to society and the educational needs of individuals growing up in that society. Given a democratic society which nevertheless retains a number of undemocratic features, some kind of experimentalist or reconstructionist approach would seem to be necessary. Reconstructionism assumes that education should be used not simply for the benefit of individuals, but also to improve a society which is capable of development. A reconstructionist curriculum will be a common or a national curriculum, but not a uniform curriculum, the details of which will be open to debate and will change from time to time.

Education, Training and the Problem 2 of Objectives

One of the problems of modern industrial society is that work tends to take on a very powerful, even dominant, significance for adults. Employers, parents and the young themselves often see childhood and adolescence largely in terms of preparation for work. This must be an incomplete view of education and maturation, since work is only one of many features of the adult world. A real danger is that preparation for work is seen as *the* purpose of education rather than one of several purposes; a related danger is that the distinction between education and training becomes blurred, or that training is confused with education completely.

In recent years there has been a good deal of discussion about education and training, sometimes contrasting the two words, sometimes treating them as synonymous. It has even been suggested that schools are failing because they are not providing the kind of trained manpower needed by industry and commerce. This is an over-simplified argument which becomes even more misleading when interpreted as an excuse for more training but less education.

In any discussion of curriculum planning it is important to preserve the distinction between the two concepts, and to emphasise that some worthwhile activities and experiences in schools may be a mixture of both. It is also important to avoid the simplistic assertion that education is good and training is inferior. The difficulty is compounded, in English, by the verb 'teach' being associated with education, whilst the verb 'instruct' is used in the context of training.

Training is the appropriate word when we are concerned with a specific skill or set of skills where there is a clear criterion or set of criteria for right and wrong. The army employs weapon training instructors, not weapon education teachers. They have clear criteria about how to hold a rifle, how to aim, how to squeeze (not pull) the trigger, how to strip and clean a rifle and so on. There is no room for any kind of debate about methods or opinions – there is a right way and a wrong way. Successful performance can easily be measured – how many bulls were scored etc. Training is a closed system; progress takes place within a deficit model – errors and omissions are easily identified and put right. A one hundred per cent success rate is the required goal. Education, on the other hand, is open-ended. Objectives cannot be defined or pre-specified with complete precision; there are criteria to indicate good and bad procedures and practices, but there will not necessarily be one correct answer, nor one right way of performing. Good performance and achievement can be recognised, perhaps even measured, but with less precision and certainty. Indeed, one of the goals of education is to encourage tolerance of

9

uncertainty and ambiguity, where appropriate. If a student stated that the French Revolution started in 1815, he is certainly wrong (although there is a good deal of doubt about when it really did start); and if we move on to the causes of the French Revolution, there is even more room for debate. There is no right answer – partly because important events in history can rarely be related to one single 'cause'. Similarly, in English literature, who can say that Olivier's interpretation of Hamlet was more 'correct' than Gielgud's? But words like 'interpretation', 'taste', 'style' are much more difficult to cope with than rifle shots hitting a target.

Although education is necessarily concerned with 'high level' activities, training is still an important aspect of educational planning. Training is a vital part of many valuable school activities. It is true that you can train a dog but not educate it; but most travellers would prefer to go to America in an aeroplane with a well-trained pilot rather than a well-educated one. Some kinds of essential training are very complex and demanding. It has become fashionable to talk of teacher education rather than teacher training, but that should not obscure the fact that for some aspects of teacher preparation, the word training might be more appropriate. Teachers, unlike pilots, need to be well-educated as well as well-trained. Most involved in higher education would like to believe that the airline pilot would be a better human being if he were educated as well as trained. Training is, however, morally neutral whereas education implies improvement in quality: it is possible to train an individual to be an efficient torturer, but you could not make him better educated in that way.

For some educational processes training is a prerequisite; schools are necessarily concerned with training as part of the education process. For example, elementary reading and arithmetic involve training in basic skills; so does learning a modern language or playing the piano. One legitimate criticism of some schools is that they do not pay enough attention to skills and training – they take them for granted when they should be more aware of them as desirable objectives; but it is equally mistaken to think of all education simply as acquiring a list of skills.

Similarly, there is a view of education and curriculum planning (in my view completely misguided) which suggests that you can reduce all learning processes to a series of *behavioural* objectives, master them as a result of training, and measure progress in terms of performance outcomes. If this were true, education as well as training could be reduced to a simple mechanistic formula. That mechanistic approach can be traced back to Franklin Bobbitt (1918) in the USA. His method was 'activity analysis':

Developed by Franklin Bobbitt and W. W. Charters, the method activity analysis came to be cloaked as the scientific way to build a curriculum. According to Bobbitt, life consists of the performance of specific activities; if education is preparation for life, then it must prepare for these specific activities; these activities, however numerous, are definite and particularised, and can be taught; therefore, these activities will be the objectives of the curriculum.

(Tanner and Tanner, 1980)

Curriculum building was, for Bobbitt, the job of an 'educational engineer', (Bobbitt, 1924). He was attempting to apply to education the techniques of the industrial psychologist F. W. (Speedy) Taylor. The approach rested on an assumption that each area of 'life activity' consisted of specifiable components. Even if that had been true and it had been possible to translate those components into a curriculum, such educational engineering would have resulted in a completely static system; there was no allowance for social change in the system. Bobbitt also intended that educational goals and standards should be set, not by teachers and educationists, but by businessmen. When Bobbitt applied activity analysis and job analysis to curriculum construction, he estimated that what schools needed to teach could be reduced to between 20 000 and 30 000 specific mechanical skills. That was a time when behaviourist psychology was in vogue, providing a convenient but false theoretical prop for the Bobbitt curriculum. Such a formula was not an attractive proposition for schools and was never seriously implemented on a wide scale, but has been revived from time to time as a 'corrective' to current educational practices.

It was not until the late 1940s that a less extreme version of the objectives approach once again came into prominence. Tyler (1949) suggested four fundamental questions to be answered in connection with any curriculum:

1 What educational purposes should the school seek to attain?
2 What educational experiences can be provided that are likely to attain these purposes?
3 How can these educational experiences be effectively organised?
4 How can we determine whether these purposes are being attained?

Tanner and Tanner (1980) have pointed out that these questions were not original, but we owe to Tyler the clarification of what is now known as the 'Tyler rationale'. Tyler's book was very influential; but it is important to distinguish between what Tyler wrote and what has been put forward by other curriculum theorists such as Mager (1962) and Popham (1969).

Mager (1962), in his work on programmed learning, demanded that objectives should be specified operationally at definite levels of performance; he then extended his demand to cover any educational intents or goals: 'Curriculum objectives must always be prespecified in terms of measureable changes in student behaviour'. We shall see that this change from objectives (Tyler) to behavioural objectives (Mager) has been of considerable significance in the debate about curriculum objectives. Popham (1969), although sometimes appearing to disagree with some of Mager's excesses, also limited the meaning of objectives to behavioural objectives. This narrow definition is similar to Bobbitt's wish to separate means and ends, that is, instruction and curriculum – the end (the curriculum) always being stated as a change in student behaviour.

Other curriculum theorists such as Hilda Taba (1962) used 'objectives' in a much wider sense, but by the early 1970s there was a powerful movement among US curriculum theorists demanding that the only meaningful interpretation of objectives was to emphasise *behavioural* objectives. Numbers of educationists appeared at curriculum conferences with lapel badges and car stickers with slogans such as 'Help stamp out non-behavioural objectives'.

Tyler himself had never adopted such a position, and in 1973 he returned to the debate criticising extremist versions of his rationale: in particular, he complained about the failure to 'distinguish between the learning of highly specific skills for limited job performance and the more generalised understanding, problem-solving skills and other kinds of behavioural patterns that thoughtful teachers and educators seek to help students develop'. (Tyler, 1973)

Many writers have objected to the behavioural objectives approach to curriculum and to the kind of behaviourist psychology associated with it. Another criticism is that many theorists tend to take existing objectives for granted rather than to submit them to critical scrutiny. Curriculum developers often define their task as improving the efficiency of existing programmes, rather than seeking to justify them or to revise them by a consideration of basic principles. Kliebard (1970), for example, stated that Tyler's treatment of educational objectives was no more than a description of the status quo when what was required was a critical analysis of Tyler's three sources of objectives – 'learners, contemporary life and subject specialists'. It is interesting to note that Tyler's three sources of objectives can be related to the three approaches identified in the discussion of ideologies in Chapter 1 – the child-centred, society-centred and knowledge-centred. But no attempt was made by Tyler to evaluate their relative importance or to judge specific inputs from any one source. Tyler's three-fold description was an acceptance of the educational status quo and an inadequate analysis of it. Tyler (1949) accepted that curriculum inputs from the three sources had to be checked against an acceptable philosophy, but the philosophy is not made clear:

> To say that educational objectives are drawn from one's philosophy... is only to say that one must make choices about educational objectives in some way related to one's value structure. This is to say so little about the process of selecting objectives as to be virtually meaningless. One wonders whether the longstanding insistence by curriculum theorists that the first step in making a curriculum be the specification of objectives has any merit whatsoever. (Kliebard, 1970)

Stenhouse and others attacked the behavioural objectives view for a different reason. Stenhouse (1970) opposed the view that an objective should be stated in terms of a student's behavioural change rather than in terms of an activity to be carried out by a teacher. Stenhouse rejected the assumption that teachers should always know exactly what response would be appropriate for every student, and also rejected the related assumptions about the nature of knowledge.

An equally strong objection may be levelled against behaviourism and behaviourist psychology. B.F. Skinner (1968) has been criticised for reducing pupils to mechanical objects and devaluing the work of teachers. Skinner described the teacher's role in purely mechanical terms: the teacher is one who 'arranges the contingencies of reinforcement' by which pupils are automatically conditioned for prespecified behavioural changes. This mechanistic and atomistic view of human life is dangerously utopian, and treats the education of human beings as if it were the same as training Skinner's pigeons.

The major mistake of those curriculum theorists basing their planning on behavioural objectives was that they tried to make this model apply to the whole of the curriculum rather than to parts of it. Because the behavioural objectives model worked well for teaching typewriting, some theorists made the simplistic assumption that it would work equally well for all educational processes. They ignored the difference between education and training and were misled by behaviourist psychologists into underestimating the complex nature of human learning. There is also more than a suspicion that the behavioural objectives model was related to a narrow, industrial concept of education concerned with job training and conformity rather than improving the quality of life.

There is, therefore, a need to distinguish objectives from behavioural objectives. Whereas it is clearly unrealistic and even dangerous to attempt to plan to whole curriculum in terms of behavioural objectives with prespecified measurable outcomes, the rational alternative is not a programme lacking any goals, specific purposes or even objectives which are less narrowly defined. It is important for teachers and students to 'know where they are going' and the conversion of general aims into objectives is a useful way of clarifying the learning process, setting realistic learning tasks, and relating learning to achievement by an assessment process with helpful feedback for the learner.

Skilbeck (1984), who is not sympathetic to behaviourism, suggests that is is useful for a curriculum to be planned in terms of objectives (that is learning activities or outcomes) rather than simply to employ very general statements about teacher intentions. Such objectives could be nearer to the closed model of training, or could be much more open, for example, concerned with understanding key concepts or ideas.

We can agree that student performances (*a*) cannot or should not be prespecified in detail and (*b*) are a part but not the whole of what we mean by education, but why should either of these considerations be inconsistent with stating objectives as the directions in which we are trying to guide student learnings?

The translation of broad aims into directions and structures for student learning is just what curriculum design is about. One of the reasons why there is so much justifiable dissatisfaction with schooling is that for large numbers of students this process is still missing out on what is important and valuable for them: by refusing to focus on sound objectives for all may we not be countenancing the continuance of an unfair and inadequate education system?... broadly based, comprehensive objectives in the curriculum need not be confused with detailed inventories of pieces of behaviour. (Skilbeck, 1984)

Curriculum planning is essentially a process of breaking down and then building up: translating broad general aims into a series of shorter-term experiences, wherever possible in a helpful sequence; then by means of a related assessment programme with regular feedback to the learner, the fragments of learning are built up once again into a whole learning experience. If that sounds too much like an automatic mechanistic exercise (what Maurice Holt, 1983, likened to 'painting by numbers') then we should remember that the experience will be slightly different for every student. It is in this way that the curriculum plan is linked to the art of the teacher in dealing with individual differences. In that context the idea of negotiated objectives becomes meaningful within the framework of a common curriculum. The learning process must be coherent for every student, but it is unlikely that coherence can be achieved in exactly the same way for a whole class. This discussion has taken us away from the problem of planning a national curriculum to the problem of school-based implementation of the curriculum plan and the role of the individual teacher.

Thus it is necessary, as Skilbeck points out, to insert a stage in the planning process before objectives:

Analyse the situation

↓

Define objectives

↓

Design the teaching-learning programme

↓

Interpret and implement the programme

↓

Assess and evaluate

This is not only a refinement of Tyler's four questions, it is also an acknowledgment that Kliebard (1970) was correct in his criticism of the Tyler rationale.

But *how* to analyse the situation? In Chapter 3, I suggest that one possible approach to this is to define curriculum as a selection from the culture of a society; curriculum planning then becomes a question of cultural *analysis* – applying values to the culture of a particular society at a particular point in time, in order to arrive at a list of cultural priorities for schools to deal with by means of the curriculum.

SUMMARY

The behaviourist view of human beings, and the behavioural objectives model of curriculum have been examined and rejected. Both views are philosophically and psychologically unsound and anti-humanistic. The behavioural objectives approach can only be applied to certain kinds of skills, not the whole curriculum. The behavioural objectives view of curriculum is that of a closed system, whereas in a democracy individuals need to become autonomous by means of an open-ended curriculum. One of the purposes of the curriculum is to encourage 'tolerance of ambiguity and uncertainty' rather than simply 'knowing the right answers'. Curriculum planning needs to maintain a distinction between education and training, although the school curriculum will include many kinds of useful training. It is impossible to begin a process of curriculum planning by making a list of statements of objectives; curriculum planning has to begin by a means of justifying value-choices. One system of making such choices will be examined in the next chapter.

3 | CULTURAL ANALYSIS

A major difference between animal behaviour and human behaviour is that human beings rely less on instinct than on learning. A bird does not need to learn how to build a nest, but humans do have to learn how to use tools, how to use language, how to know what is appropriate or inappropriate behaviour, and many other aspects of culture. The disadvantage of this is that children are dependent on their parents or other adults for many years; on the other hand, human behaviour is much more flexible and adaptive: we do not have to do exactly what the previous generation did, but can make changes. Thus social change is a feature of human communities but not of animal groups.

CULTURE

The word 'culture' as used by social scientists means everything that is created by human beings themselves: tools and technology, language and literature, music and art, science and mathematics, attitudes and values – in effect, the whole way of life of a society. Culture, as defined by Linton (1940), is 'the sum total of the knowledge, attitudes and habitual behaviour patterns shared and transmitted by the members of a particular society'.

Any society has the problem of passing on this way of life, or culture, to the next generation. In simple societies culture is transmitted directly by members of the family or by means of other 'face to face' relations. In complex societies, the division of labour and social mobility make it impossible for culture to be passed on by traditional, informal means, and the task is partly entrusted to formal education.

Education is concerned with making available to the next generation what we regard as the most valuable aspects of culture. Because schools have limited time and resources, the curriculum needs to be planned to ensure that an appropriate selection from culture is made. Those responsible for making the selection have a duty to demonstrate that it is neither arbitrary nor idiosyncratic; it should be open to rational enquiry and justification, not least because complete agreement about the curriculum will rarely be possible.

In order to plan a curriculum based on a justifiable selection from culture, it is necessary to have a process or set of principles by which it can be seen that the selection is being made. That process will be referred to as 'cultural analysis'. The rest of this chapter will include an outline of a cultural analysis process which cannot claim to be 'value-free', but can claim to state values explicitly. 'Justification' takes place in a context of values, some of which may be well-established societal values enshrined in legislation (such as equal opportunity), others will be more basic human values common to all societies, and some may be values which in a pluralist society may be seen as more controversial – but still open to rational enquiry.

CULTURAL ANALYSIS AND CULTURAL MAPPING

There are two possible approaches to cultural analysis: the classificatory and the interpretative. The classificatory method would involve checklists, tables and elaborate statistical systems. The interpretative approach is concerned with looking at the culture as a whole.

Some anthropologists have attempted elaborate systems of classification of simple societies by listing and categorising key characteristics such as kinship, economic features or religious beliefs. The danger in this approach is of being so concerned with the accumulation of detail that generalisation becomes impossible. On the other hand, it is equally possible for anthropologists to misinterpret a society by relying on dominant impressions and reaching conclusions too easily.

The educationist analysing his own society has some advantages over the anthropologist in a strange community: he is unlikely to be so completely misled as some anthropologists seem to have been by native informants; but he has to be aware of the problem of analysing his own society through his own ideology or belief system. He may take some aspects of culture for granted which ought to be questioned, and he may assume the value of practices which ought to be doubted. Part of the answer is that anyone attempting this kind of cultural analysis has to learn to stand back from society and try to see it as much as possible as 'an outsider'. The observer can never be value-free, but he can learn to become more aware of his own values, beliefs and prejudices.

MEASUREMENT OR INTERPRETATION?

Some aspects of culture can be measured (for example, some economic features of industrial societies), but observers should avoid the temptation to measure what is easily quantifiable and then place too much importance on those measures. Much of cultural analysis has to be at the level of impressionistic description:

The concept of culture I espouse...is essentially a semiotic one. Believing, that man is an animal suspended in webs of significance he himself has spun, I take culture to be those webs and the analysis of it to be, therefore, not an experimental science in search of law, but an interpretative one in search of meaning. (Geertz, 1975)

It will sometimes be necessary to be more specific than Geertz suggests, and to ask detailed questions about knowledge, skills and values; but it will always be important to retain that interpretative view of culture. If we try to reduce a culture to tables and checklists, we run the risk of over-simplification. But there may be times when tables and checklists will have a limited usefulness.

At the simplest level, cultural analysis for the purpose of curriculum planning would ask:

1   What kind of society already exists?
2   In what ways is it developing?
3   How do its members appear to want it to develop?
4   What kind of values and principles will be involved in deciding on this 'development' as well as the educational means of achieving it?

In the process of cultural analysis it is helpful to view culture as an historical as well as a contemporary process: not only to 'take a snapshot' of culture now, but also to see how it has developed. In educational analysis, we must look for culture lag and curriculum inertia: there is a tendency for schools to lag behind other aspects of social and cultural change, and for the curriculum to become irrelevant. This is not to fall into the trap of identifying 'educational needs' with technological advance nor to equate education with vocational training; but there is a tendency for curricula to get out of date unless efforts are made to counter the natural conservatism of schools.

A selection from the culture is thus made by analysing society and 'mapping out' the kind of knowledge and experiences that are most appropriate for the development of the society. Three kinds of classification are needed: first, deciding on major parameters – the cultural invariants or human universals; second, outlining a method of analysis to describe any society making use of those parameters – that is, moving from cultural invariants to cultural variables; third, a means of classifying the educationally desirable knowledge and experiences.

This is to deviate from the traditional approach to curriculum planning: in the past, much discussion took place about the classification of knowledge (for example, Hirst (1975) and Phenix (1964)) but little attention was paid to the analysis of society, and deriving from that analysis an account of the kinds of knowledge and experiences needed by the young at various stages in their development.

A diagrammatic outline of this approach, represented as a series of five sequential stages is set out on the next page (Figure 1). As a model and, therefore, as a simplified guide to action, it could be used at any level of curriculum planning: for example, for drawing up national guidelines, at the level of school planning, or by an individual teacher making a deliberate choice of teaching materials: 19

Figure 1   *Curriculum: a selection from culture*

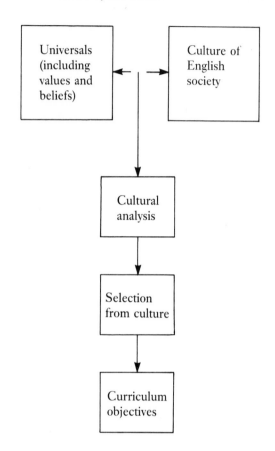

HUMAN UNIVERSALS/CULTURAL INVARIANTS

Anthropologists such as Ruth Benedict (1934) have emphasised differences between societies; others such as Clyde Kluckhohn (1949) and Dorothy Lee (1960) have stressed the essential similarities between all societies. My purpose is to begin the analysis by looking at the characteristics that all human beings appear to have in common (the human universals/cultural invariants) within the Kluckhohn tradition, and then to analyse at a later stage how these are or should be related to education.

In analysing cultures I suggest that we concentrate on nine major headings describing groups of cultural invariants. It is not suggested that the nine sub-systems are exhaustive, and culture could be sub-classified in a variety of ways, but there are good sociological reasons for suggesting that no society could exist if it lacked any one of the following nine sub-systems, although it might be the case that some of them are more important than others in industrial societies from the point of view of formal education. In other words, a society could not exist without any one of the nine, but it is perfectly possible to imagine an education service, without one – provided that the system were transmitted by other means.

The nine cultural invariants or cultural sub-systems are as follows:

1 Socio-political system
2 Economic system
3 Communication system
4 Rationality system
5 Technology system
6 Morality system
7 Belief system
8 Aesthetic system
9 Maturation system

1 Socio-political system

All societies have some kind of social structure, that is, a system of defining relationships within the society as a whole. Kinship, status, role, duty and obligation are the key social concepts which not only exist in every society but have to be passed on to the next generation.

In some societies, social structure is simple and taken for granted; in others, the system is complex and open to change. The socio-political system will be closely related to economic and technological factors: for example, when Western European societies were largely rural and agricultural, the dominant political factor was the possession of land; but as trade and industry developed, land ownership became less important than the ownership of the means of production. There are various ways of classifying societies: for example, social stratification is usually important, and in industrial societies social class is highly significant. Power and authority are important concepts; the family and other social institutions always exist in some form.

2 Economic system

Every society has some means of dealing with the problem of scarce resources, their distribution and exchange. In some societies, the economy will be simple, in others such as Western industrial societies, they are extremely complex. There are various ways of analysing economic systems, about which countless books have been written. One important differentiating factor is the division of labour and the amount of specialisation that exists; this is connected with concepts such as work, leisure and the market. In most societies money, credit and other ideas associated with wealth, income, buying and spending will grow in complexity as the society becomes more industrialised and moves further away from simple systems of economic exchange.

Most adults in modern industrial societies have only a very hazy idea about their own economic system and how it works.

3 Communication system

One of the major differences between human beings and other animals is the existence of language and the greater degree of complexity in communication that this affords. Where communication is entirely by means of spoken language, much of the learning required is informal – children and their parents need not be aware that language learning is constantly taking place. In those societies where written language is developed, two changes take place: first, writing has to be consciously learned; second, those who acquire writing skills are at an advantage over the 'illiterate'. The invention of print is also of considerable social significance. Printed texts make specialised knowledge available but, at the same time, increase the differences between the educated and the uneducated. In pre-literate societies age, experience and 'memory' are valued much more than they are in those societies where records are easily kept. Thus the communication system is related to the socio-political system in important ways, as well as to rationality (see below).

Communication consists of more than language: many kinds of signs, symbols and signalling systems have to be learned by each generation.

4 Rationality system

All societies are rational in the sense of having a view about what is reasonable and what counts as an explanation. The kinds of explanation will differ from time to time and from place to place, but human beings always attempt to explain physical phenomena and human behaviour. The system of rationality is closely linked with the communication system; words and other signs must be used consistently to make comprehension and cooperation possible.

Levi-Strauss (1966) has classified societies as 'hot' societies characterised by scientific thinking, and 'cold' (primitive) societies which are 'time-suppressing' and rely on myth rather than science and history to explain their universe.

5 Technology system

Human beings in all societies have developed tools to build shelters, to produce food and to improve the quality of life in other ways. All human beings are 'technologists' in the sense of being users and makers of tools. The process of learning to use tools is always an important feature of cultural life. The system of technology will range from the very simple, where every member of society can master the whole of the technology, to the very complex where no one individual can ever understand all of it. The complexity of the technology system poses problems for cultural transmission: specialisation and division of labour have repercussions on the socio-political and the economic systems.

6 Morality system

All human beings a moral animals. All societies have some kind of code of behaviour, and make distinctions between right and wrong. What is regarded as appropriate in one society may be very different from the rules operating in another place or time. In some societies the moral code is unitary and taken for granted; in others, value pluralism exists and the problem of transmitting morality to the young will become more difficult.

7 Belief system

Every society will have a dominant belief system. In some, beliefs are predominantly of a religious kind, perhaps based on divine revelation. In others, beliefs may be derived from creation myths. In Western industrial societies, religious beliefs have become weaker, but have not disappeared altogether; nevertheless, sociologists talk about such societies as being secularised, where 'man is the measure of all things' and scientific explanations occupy a dominant position.

8 Aesthetic system

All human beings have aesthetic drives and needs. Every society produces some kind of art and entertainment, even when living close to subsistence level. If a society makes cooking pots, there will be a tendency to decorate them, and where decoration exists, standards will develop. One of the interesting features of human life is the range of aesthetic forms, but in no society is a sense of 'beauty' absent.

9 Maturation system

Every society has a set of customs and conventions concerned with 'growing up'. Anthropologists have written extensively on the variety of child-rearing practices which exist or have existed. In some societies the transition from childhood to an adult role is marked by rituals and ceremonies indicating a clear-cut change of status; in others, there may be a vague, ill-defined period of adolescence.

All societies have activities associated with stages of development: children play whilst adults work or hunt (although the concepts play and work may not exist as such). Growth, maturity and ageing are treated differently in various societies, but there are always important customs to be observed. In some developed industrial societies, the problems of transition may be considerable, partly because no clear rules are available.

SUMMARY

I have attempted to analyse briefly those characteristics which all human societies have in common. Any human group which did not possess all of those nine systems could not be considered to be a 'society'. No anthropologist has ever found a group of human beings living permanently together lacking any one of those nine characteristic systems.

A society not only possesses the nine systems but must also have some means of transmitting these systems from one generation to the next. Some societies will achieve this cultural transmission partly by means of formal education. It will be the responsibility of schools to pass on all these aspects of culture, unless there are other agencies available for that purpose.

The argument is deliberately circular: if curriculum is defined as a selection from culture, then the selection must be an adequate one; culture can be sub-divided into nine systems, so an adequate selection will include all nine, unless we can be assured that the necessary transmission takes place outside schooling.

The next stage of cultural analysis will involve applying those nine sub-systems to our own society. Such a description provides the basis for cultural mapping, giving a more detailed picture of those features of contemporary culture which should be represented in the school curriculum. Part of that stage of planning will be to examine existing curricula in terms of the description of society derived from the analysis.

4 | CULTURAL ANALYSIS APPLIED TO CONTEMPORARY ENGLAND

In Chapter 3, curriculum was defined as a selection from culture; culture was sub-divided, for purposes of analysis, into nine cultural systems. In this chapter each of the nine will be applied to contemporary England. In order to avoid proceeding through the nine systems for a third time, after each description of a system applied to England today, comparisons will be made between what exists in the culture and what is reflected (or omitted) in school curricula.

At this stage I also want to introduce another feature of the analysis: in the course of analysing contemporary English culture and comparing it with school curricula, some *cultural contradictions* will be detected. These contradictions are important not only for social reasons, but for their curricular implications. For example, the idea of equality of opportunity is contradicted by the continued existence of the privilege of having the right to buy access to certain kinds of education. The study of cultural contradictions has not received enough attention from the socio-educational point of view. Marx and Weber referred to contradictions in more general terms; Tawney (1931) referred to social justice and class in England with particular reference to education. Some writers have discussed the problem in terms of hypocrisy; others, such as Edmund King (1979), have referred to paradoxes. These are features of many societies, but several writers have drawn particular attention to the cultural contradictions within English society. As well as contradictions, attention will also be drawn to gaps in the curriculum, and to 'mismatches' between what is and what ought to be in the curriculum.

1 SOCIO-POLITICAL SYSTEM

Many volumes have been written about the English social structure and its political system. The following account is necessarily only a very brief summary.

England is a large, densely populated, urban industrial society with growing problems of social control: crime, juvenile delinquency, vandalism and general unrest among the young are on the increase. It would appear that the problem of how to cope with young people growing up in an industrial society, especially in overcrowded inner cities, has been seriously under-estimated. Added to these problems, in recent years there have been additional difficulties of accommodating immigrant minorities resulting in a series of crises – social, political and educational as well as economic.

An important factor complicating the problem of urban industrial society is social class. Class influences and sometimes dominates other aspects of social life, including education and industry. The 'old boy network' is more powerful in England than in Japan, Germany or the USA. Despite the fact that the class structure retains feudal vestiges such as the House of Lords, the monarchy, titles and so on, England claims to be a democratic and open society. This is one of the cultural contradictions referred to above. Ideals such as equal opportunity are enshrined in legislation but the ideal is far from the reality.

England is a complex urban society with a very elaborate political and social structure. However, most young people leave school almost entirely ignorant of the socio-political system. England is an industrialised society, but education has failed to enable the young to live harmoniously within that society. They have an imperfect understanding of industrialisation; many are not educated in such a way as to gain employment or to be able to cope with unemployment. England is a democratic society with a high rate of social mobility, but schools tend to divide the young socially, academically and culturally, rather than to encourage cooperation, social harmony and the development of a common culture.

These are a few of the cultural contradictions connected with the socio-political system which clearly overlap with some of the other eight systems. As well as indicating contradictions, any comparison of contemporary English culture with existing school curricula will show up gaps and mismatches. Part of the gap-filling exercise would be to suggest that no secondary school curriculum should be regarded as satisfactory unless it contains a reasonable amount of time devoted to the social sciences, including a suitable programme of political literacy. This recommendation has been made by Her Majesty's Inspectorate (HMI) on several occasions (DES 1977c, 1981a). As well as the problems of gaps in the curriculum there is the related problem of 'mismatch': schools who pay lip-service to the need for social and political education by what Americans often refer to as 'Mickey Mouse' social studies – for example, programmes which include much detail about 'how a Bill becomes an Act' but avoids most of the potentially controversial issues.

2 ECONOMIC SYSTEM

England is an industrialised society experiencing great difficulty in retaining its place among the most developed and prosperous nations. It relies heavily on the ability to export manufactured goods in order to pay for imports, including food. Only about one third of food is home-grown, and it is doubtful whether the country could support its large population by growing more food.

Not only is England a highly industrialised society, it was the first country to experience the Industrial Revolution. This gave England economic advantages in the eighteenth and nineteenth centuries which have now become disadvantages. Other countries have learned the lessons of later phases of industrialisation more easily than England which is handicapped by its pre-industrial social structure and attitudes (Barnett, 1986). In addition, England faced the difficulties of ceasing to be an imperial power with captive markets and easy sources of cheap raw materials.

One striking feature of English society is that it no longer finds it easy to earn a living: imports exceed exports in most years, despite the very great contribution made by service industries, banking and insurance as invisible exports. Unemployment is high, despite a shortage of skilled labour.

Another feature of the English economic system is that it is a capitalist system which has succeeded in withstanding many of the advances of welfare state socialism and, in recent years, recovering some of the lost ground by encouraging programmes of privatisation or denationalisation. The English version of a mixed economy combined with multi-national capitalism allows a good deal of wealth and power to remain within the control of 'the ruling class'.

There are two major educational implications emerging from this analysis. The first is the need for the young to understand the economic system; the second, is the assertion that the curriculum should enable school-leavers to take part in 'the world of work'.

The first is easy to accept but may be difficult to accommodate within existing timetables. Most young people leave school with little understanding of the economic system. Economics is taught in many schools but tends to be an option rather than part of a common curriculum. The curriculum should be replanned so that all young people leave school with an understanding of such concepts as supply and demand, the market, exports and imports and so on.

The second implication is that schools should prepare the young for the economic system. If this means that schools should enable young people to earn a living, then there can be little objection to that. If, however, it is suggested that an important function of the curriculum is to supply industry with docile manpower, then ideological difficulties may emerge. A distinction needs to be made between the general education of the young, which would include education for work, and narrow vocational training. There is also a difference between sensibly adjusting the school curriculum to match economic and industrial changes (for example, by including computer studies or micro-technology) and allowing the school curriculum to be completely dominated by the supposed needs of the industry.

3 COMMUNICATION SYSTEM

It is now possible, as a result of various linguistic surveys, to state with some accuracy how many people in England speak English as their mother tongue and also to locate the hundreds of minority languages which are spoken as first or 27 second languages. It is equally possible to make accurate statements about the varieties of English, such as dialects and specialised registers. The English have a reputation for failing to respect the language customs of linguistic minorities: at various times the languages of the Welsh, the Scots and the Irish have been forbidden. More recently, the linguistic difficulties of immigrants have not been treated with very great sympathy. Similarly, until relatively recently the existence of non-standard forms of English – working class language and some dialects – were regarded as deviant. This is not to deny, however, that all young people should have the opportunity of acquiring 'standard English' as part of their normal education.

English language is not the only form of communication. A scientific, industrialised society uses mathematics as a form of communication; in a democratic society much vital information is communicated publicly by statistical charts and diagrams; it is also suggested that everyone should become computer-literate; many symbols and signs have to be used or at least understood – for example, complex systems of road signs. The division of labour combined with the development of printing produced specialised vocabularies and other linguistic features which may make communication difficult. The existence of the mass media is also an important feature of the communication system.

English language is taken seriously as a school subject but is often taught in a limited way from the point of view of communication. Official reports from the 1920s to the Bullock Report (DES, 1975) and the Kingman Report (DES, 1988a) have diagnosed shortcomings in the teaching of English. At least two points need to be stressed: first, the neglect of oral language; second, the failure in many schools to develop a policy of language across the curriculum, that is, to treat English as more than a school subject, but as a means of communicating in a variety of ways according to subject matter. The failure to develop a policy of language across the curriculum is connected with a failure to teach various specialist forms of English – linguistic varieties such as the language of science – and also a failure to relate everyday language to the academic language of the classroom.

As for the non-language forms of communication, many schools have yet to embark upon serious programmes to deal with non-linguistic communication; adequate education in communication would also include film studies, television studies and advertising techniques. There are many curriculum gaps to be filled.

4 Rationality system

In the terminology used by Levi-Strauss, England is a 'hot' culture. It has coped with rapid social and technological change by developing a rationality which can explain change, and regards change as normal. This kind of rationality is associated historically with the Protestant Reformation of the sixteenth and seventeenth centuries which questioned traditional authority and explained the universe 'rationally'. Newtonian science provided a rule system to explain the physical universe; the *laissez-faire* economics of Adam Smith, and the utilitarian philosophy of Bentham and Mill attempted to find an equivalent scientific method to apply to human behaviour. Thus, in England the 'scientific' form of knowledge has become dominant, despite doubts about its applicability in the social sciences and the existence of other kinds of rationality in the fields of aesthetics and other kinds of human experiences.

The school curriculum normally includes 'scientific rationality' but two points need to be made: first, many children 'learn' science without understanding scientific method and scientific reasoning; second, pupils are not usually taught to distinguish scientific reasoning and other 'forms of knowledge' – for example, the different ways of thinking and feeling required in appreciating poetry, music or art.

5   TECHNOLOGY SYSTEM

In modern industrial society, technology is so complex that no individual can be expected to master the whole of it. Specialisation is inevitable. This is an advantage in some respects but aggravates the problem of differential access to knowledge. Society may become dangerously divided, for example, into those who can master computerised techniques of information retrieval, and those who simply do not know how to find out. Technology is closely related to the economic system: it is important to resolve the relationship between education, work and technology.

Although England was first into the field of industrialisation, it has never been completely acceptable for the upper classes to work in industry or become industrialists. Throughout the nineteenth century industry and commerce were seen as inferior occupations incompatible with the status of gentleman. The disastrous consequences of this attitude, which has survived to some extent, have been pointed out by Weiner (1981), Roderick and Stevens (1981), and Barnett (1986). Another interesting cultural contradiction is that although England was the first to become industrialised, the process of socialising the workers into accepting the work ethic has never been completely successful. The contrast between the attitudes of English workers and those in Hong Kong, Japan or even Western Germany is interesting. Edward Thompson (1968) has described the difficulties of disciplining the workers in the eighteenth and nineteenth centuries, and the damage caused to their cultural life, but the process was never complete. In many respects, England is still a play culture rather than a work culture. It is no coincidence that the English developed so many sports and games as well as many leisure pursuits.

Although specialisation is necessary, schools have a responsibility to enable all young people to have a general understanding of technology and its place in modern Britain (as well as to train specialists). The educational problem is   29 two-fold: it is partly a question of curriculum and partly a question of the status of technology as a kind of knowledge. Even in those schools which offer technology as a subject, it is almost without exception an option for the 14+ age group, rather than being part of the common curriculum. This will, of course, change as a result of the national curriculum proposals for technology in primary and secondary schools. It will also be necessary to ensure that adequate attention be paid to technology by other subject teachers. History teachers, for example, are often good at making the Industrial Revolution interesting, but neglect to show the historical and social importance of technological developments in nineteenth and twentieth centuries. As for the status of technology as a subject, it will be essential to encourage teachers and pupils to recognise technology as a vital feature of our culture. The technology system should also be related to the aesthetic system wherever possible.

6 MORALITY SYSTEM

England is an example of 'moral pluralism' in which a largely secular morality is dominant. It would be difficult to regard England as a Christian society, despite the continued existence of the established Church and the assumption made, for example, in the 1944 Education Act, that religion means the Christian religion. Since the Reformation, the idea of a single uncontroversial moral system has been progressively weakened: the Church split up into a number of denominations and sects; in addition, the whole notion of religious and moral authority was questioned. By the late nineteenth century a mixture of utilitarian and Christian principles provided the main basis for moral thinking, but the two were often in opposition and provided another example of a cultural contradiction. In the twentieth century, especially after World War II, immigration from non-Christian societies further complicated the moral scene. Another difficulty is that law and morality are seen as separate; a related danger is what Durkheim referred to as *anomie* – not really knowing what the rules of society are. A connected danger is the retreat to moral relativism – the idea that morality is simply a matter of taste.

The absence of systematic teaching about the moral system is perhaps the most serious gap in the curriculum. Little attempt has been made to teach elementary ethics as Dearden (1968) recommended twenty years ago. Few schools have a programme to develop the moral autonomy of pupils.

Some schools and LEAs have made more progress than others. At least one LEA has encouraged the use of tutor group time for the discussion of practical moral questions along the lines advocated by Button (1981, 1982). Others make some use of *Lifeline* materials (McPhail, 1972). It will also be necessary for individual schools to discuss what contributions other subjects, such as English and history, can make to moral development. Teachers will need some in-service education before undertaking this work. It has also been suggested (Pring, 1982) that schools should consciously attempt to become better examples of moral institutions.

7 BELIEF SYSTEM

In one respect, the problems of the belief system are similar to those of the moral system discussed above: there appears to be a lack of consensus with accompanying dangers of relativism and anomie. However, studies have shown that there is an underlying set of beliefs shared by the vast majority of the population. The belief system is a complex mixture of religious, political and scientific beliefs and values – but contradictions abound.

It has sometimes been suggested that beliefs and values should be transmitted by the family rather than through the school curriculum, but it is precisely because there are differences within society between families and other social groups that schools have a responsibility for dealing with the task from a national and international point of view, rather than a parochial attitude and achieving as much consensus as possible. In many cases, if values and beliefs are not transmitted by the school they will not be transmitted at all. Teachers in England are sometimes critical of such American practices as 'saluting the flag', but schools in the USA have been used consciously to Americanise immigrants and to inculcate the idea of 'the nation'. Schools in England have, in the past, preached patriotic values in slightly more subtle ways – there are many studies of history and geography textbooks to illustrate this. In recent years the virtues of patriotism have been called into question, and schools are more likely to try to promote 'international understanding' or 'multiculturalism'. These values are more difficult to pass on than simple patriotism, and are generally not clearly defined either as objectives or in terms of teaching methods.

There are some ideas and concepts such as democracy which tend to be 'believed in' without being understood. Schools need to work out better programmes for developing such values and beliefs, including some opportunities to practise them. It is also easier to teach the idea of tolerance than to teach the young to be more tolerant; and it is even more difficult to reach agreement on reasonable limits to toleration: at what point in a democracy should we cease to tolerate those who abuse tolerance and threaten the survival of democracy?

It is not suggested that a school should have 'belief system' on the timetable, but it is not sufficient to say that this is part of the hidden curriculum or that 'we teach it all the time'. Schools must map out the conceptual territory and the related experiences as objectives, find out to what extent they will be covered within existing subject areas, and then, having identified the gaps, make sure that coverage is completed. This point will be further discussed later in this book, in the context of the 1988 national curriculum.

8 AESTHETIC SYSTEM

The aesthetic system also presents problems for education. In the process of art being separated from religion, it was also separated from the everyday life of the majority of the population. A number of problems emerge for a society at this stage, especially where the value system is pluralistic. What counts as art is one problem; even more difficult is what counts as good art. At a time of rapid social and technological change the rules or criteria of excellence are blurred – and sometimes even appear to have been completely abandoned. Problems of the aesthetic system are related to other problems and contradictions within the social structure. What is classified as art tends to be related to the high culture of the upper and upper middle classes. For example, art correspondents rarely discuss the aesthetic qualities of cars, or furniture; the art and architecture criteria applying to public buildings are not considered appropriate to interior decorating in ordinary homes; gardening, the most pervasive art form in England, is not taken seriously except for elite landscape gardens of stately homes. The assumption is generally made that different rules apply in each of those cases. High culture and popular culture are falsely separated.

Teachers are unclear and uneasy about attitudes to 'high culture' and 'mass culture'. Attempts need to be made to clarify what the issues are in terms of aesthetic criteria and judging what is excellent. It is not enough to say that confusion is inevitable or that aesthetic questions of this kind are too difficult. Many schools also offer too limited a range of aesthetic experiences. Painting and drawing are usually available but, in many, sculpture, pottery and photography, for example, could be made available. The Gulbenkian Report (1982) *The Arts in Schools* contains a useful review of the problems.

9 MATURATION SYSTEM

In England there is a good deal of agreement about how babies should be treated, but some disagreement on the extent to which young children should be indulged or encouraged to conform. Habits have changed in the recent past and may still be subject to continuing change. The Victorian values of 'spare the rod and spoil the child' have given way to greater permissiveness, but experts as well as parents are unsure about many aspects of child rearing. (The disagreements among parents may be similar in some respects to arguments between classical humanist and progressivist educators).

In England there is no clear-cut demarcation between child and adult; instead we have a long period of adolescence clouded with doubts and uncertainties. These ambiguities are made worse by the existence of legal definitions, some of which coincide with normal experience, whereas others are meant to be legal, but not necessarily normal limits. Thus a young person is entitled to vote at 18 (and is normally expected to do so); he or she is allowed to marry at 16 (but this only means that it is not permissible to marry at a younger age); and at 17 driving a car is permitted, if a driving test is passed. Some young people begin work at 16 – an important indication of adult status – but it is increasingly common to delay that status change until 18, 21 or even older.

Play, or sport, is important at all stages. The very young are expected to play as part of their 'natural' development; older children take part in organised games; adults, especially males, are expected to take an interest in sport and preferably to participate in at least one activity. There are regional as well as social class variations in expectations and practices.

It is part of the function of education to sort out as much of the confusion as possible as well as to develop 'healthy' maturation. With the growth of industrialisation and urbanisation various state agencies, including formal schooling, have taken over some of the functions of the family, especially in the areas of health care and child rearing. Thus, there are demands to extend schooling downwards at least to age 4, partly to enable young mothers to work. The curriculum for 4-year-olds is open to dispute, as is the most appropriate programme for pre-school play groups and nursery classes; but there are also pressures to return to traditional customs – even to 'Victorian values' – on questions of upbringing (Anderson, 1988).

At a later stage of maturation, it can no longer be assumed that boys and girls will learn about child rearing within their own families: the reduced number of children in the average family makes this kind of involvement much less likely. It is often reasonably suggested that child rearing needs to be taught in schools as part of the curriculum; but health education, together with sex education, is not part of the 1988 national curriculum. It will be another aspect of school curriculum planning to ensure that these very important 'cross-curriculum' areas are included within the school programme.

Summary

In this chapter I have attempted to apply the process of cultural analysis, described in Chapter 3, to contemporary England. Each of the nine cultural systems has been used to describe aspects of English society as it now exists and as it is continuing to develop. The implications for curriculum planning have been sketched out, bearing in mind some of the cultural contradictions which continue to affect schools. The result of this analysis is, to some extent, a contrast between 'what is' and 'what ought to be' in the school curriculum. There are close links between this analysis and some of the discussion of a national curriculum which will follow in Chapters 5 and 6.

From the Secret Garden to a National Curriculum
5 (1960–88)

There are two main reasons for planning a central curriculum. First, educational reasons, for example, bringing the curriculum into line with social, technological or pedagogical changes; and second, for reasons of political control. It is of course possible for the two trends to be happening at the same time, thus making it difficult to disentangle some of the issues. Such has been the case in England since the 1960s.

The previous chapters have been concerned with the educational arguments in favour of a common or national curriculum. In 1987–88 a national curriculum was established, partly for political reasons. It will be important to precede the discussion of this version of a national curriculum (which will follow in Chapter 6), by outlining the development of the changing social and political scene which made a national curriculum possible and politically attractive at this time.

It is sometimes asserted that in England there is a long tradition of teacher control of the curriculum. This is not true. Before 1944 there were very strong central influences: elementary schools had been tightly controlled by Codes from 1862 until they were replaced by a 'Handbook of Suggestions' in 1905 which continued to act as a powerful set of curriculum guidelines; county secondary schools were centrally controlled by Regulations from 1904 onwards – immediately following the establishment of county secondary schools by the 1902 Education Act. The 1944 Education Act replaced all these controls and, whether by design or accident, the curriculum as such was not mentioned in the Education Act, and the only subject required by law was religious instruction. The Minister of Education had considerable statutory powers, but responsibility for curriculum planning was delegated to local education authorities (LEAs) who, having major problems of buildings and staffing to contend with, left it to the schools themselves. Thus began the 'golden age' of teacher control of the curriculum, although there were always constraining influences such as examinations, HMI, governors and parents. Teacher control remained throughout the 1950s, partly because the other two 'partners' – LEAs and the Ministry – were preoccupied with organisational issues, and partly because the curriculum did not appear to be in any way contentious. It was taken for granted that education was worthwhile for individuals and for society, and that benefits would flow automatically from the policy of secondary education for all. Some assumed that the curriculum for all secondary pupils would necessarily be a version of the 1904 secondary school curriculum; others wanted to free the new secondary modern schools from the burden of examinations. There was, however, little or no national debate, political

35

or educational, about primary and secondary curricula.

The first manifestation of a centralist move to influence curriculum came in the early 1960s. David Eccles, the Conservative Minister of Education, debating the Crowther Report in the House of Commons in 1960, expressed regret that debates on education were devoted to bricks and mortar and matters of organisation rather than the content of the curriculum. He said that it was his intention to 'make the Ministry's voice heard rather more often and positively and no doubt controversially' (Manzer, 1970). Eccles used the phrase 'secret garden of the curriculum' to indicate his dislike of an important area being closed to open discussion. He established the innocuous Curriculum Study Group in 1962, but it was tactlessly described as a 'commando-type unit'. The other partners (teachers and LEAs) expressed their alarm, and jointly opposed this new centralism to such an extent that in 1963 a new Minister of Education, Sir Edward Boyle, reacted by setting up the Lockwood Committee to establish a more acceptable body. In 1964 this resulted in the Schools Council for Curriculum and Examinations.

The teachers and the LEAs had won the battle but not the war. Teachers demanded and were given a majority on most important Schools Council committees. The Schools Council was independent of the central authority, being jointly funded by LEAs and the recently reorganised Department of Education and Science (DES). It has, however, been suggested that the teaching profession did not make the most of this opportunity, and that the Schools Council made a major mistake by not tackling the question of a national curriculum; instead they continued with their doctrine that curriculum planning was the concern of individual schools. The Schools Council was responsible for a good deal of excellent research and development, but it adopted a deliberately piecemeal approach which ignored the central question of the curriculum as a whole.

Throughout the later 1960s and 1970s, criticisms of schools intensified, many of them being concerned with progressive methods and curriculum innovation associated with the Schools Council. The first of the Black Papers (Cox and Dyson, 1969) appeared in 1969, attacking 'progressive' and comprehensive education. The question of standards in schools increasingly became a matter of public concern, and in 1974 the DES set up the Assessment of Performance Unit (APU) as a way of providing evidence on standards. In 1976 a newly appointed Permanent Secretary at the DES, James Hamilton, publicly questioned the lack of attention paid to complaints about education, and criticised teachers for sheltering behind their expertise. In the same year, arguments about the curriculum being too important to be left to teachers came from the political left as well as the right. Ann Corbett, (1976) suggested that reformed governing bodies, including parents, ought to exercise more influence on the curriculum; Timothy Raison, a moderate Conservative, argued that the 1944 Education Act should have included curriculum guidelines (Raison, 1976).

In 1976 the 10th Report of the House of Commons Expenditure Committee criticised the DES, complaining that the DES officials confused resource allocation with educational planning. In the same year the Organisation for Economic Cooperation and Development (OECD) reported on the DES, making much the same kind of criticism about the lack of central policy in education. In October 1976 the Labour Prime Minister, James Callaghan, made a speech at Ruskin College, in Oxford, and implicitly criticised schools for failing to provide suitable manpower for a modern industrial society. Part of his briefing for the Ruskin speech was the famous 'Yellow Book' – a supposedly secret document prepared by the DES for the Prime Minister, and deliberately leaked to the press; it was critical of schools and of the Schools Council. Throughout 1976 there was also a good deal of public discussion and press coverage of the William Tyndale School scandal; in 1977 the Auld Report was published, which revealed that a group of teachers had been allowed to remain in control of a school with a grossly inadequate curriculum; the DES and HMI had regarded this as an LEA problem.

Prime Minister Callaghan's Ruskin speech initiated the Great Debate on education, which included some discussion of the curriculum. A Green Paper *Education in Schools* (DES, 1977a) was published containing a forthright statement reaffirming the Secretary of State's responsibilities for the curriculum. It was proposed that LEAs should carry out a review, in consultation with their teachers and report on curriculum policies. This request was officially made in DES Circular 14/77 'LEA Arrangements for the School Curriculum'. When LEA responses were eventually received, the DES indicated that they were not satisfied with what the LEAs were, or rather were not, doing in connection with curriculum planning: a report was published on the responses to Circular 14/77 *Local Authority Arrangements for the School Curriculum:Report on the Circular 14/77* (DES, 1979b). It was alleged that LEAs were not in possession of adequate information about curriculum planning within their schools, and many LEAs had no satisfactory policy on curriculum.

In 1979 there was a change of government – the beginning of Margaret Thatcher's Conservative administration. Although this political change has had important long-term effects on education, it would be wrong to see 1979 as representing a complete change of policy in education: in some respects the emerging centralism simply continued to develop. In January 1980 the DES published a document on curriculum clearly intending to put right some of the inadequacies detected after the issue of Circular 14/77. *A Framework for the School Curriculum* (DES, 1980a) was an openly centralist discussion document, suggesting not only a subject based core curriculum, but with time allocations attached. This approach was attacked by teachers and other educationists for its bureaucratic and technicist style, and a modified version was published in the following year *The School Curriculum* (DES, 1981c). This was followed by two more Circulars calling for LEA action on curriculum: Circular 6/81 and Circular 8/83, each calling the attention of LEAs to their responsibilities for curriculum policy and curriculum control. LEAs were firmly being instructed to get to grips with the problem of curriculum planning, but they were experiencing considerable difficulties in producing the kind of answers the DES wanted.

Meanwhile, another group of educationists were making a bid to exert influence over the school curriculum. In the early 1970s the Curriculum Publication Group within HMI were discussing and writing about a common curriculum. In

December 1977 they provided a very important document *Curriculum 11–16* (DES, 1977c). HMI were critical of the curricular arrangements of many secondary schools, in particular the option systems for the 14–16 age group. HMI argued that a worthwhile curriculum should be regarded as a right of young people, and set out what they regarded as a desirable common curriculum (later referred to as an entitlement curriculum) for all pupils up to the age of 16. The recommended curriculum was based not on subjects but on 'areas of experience'. Unfortunately, throughout this period there seemed to be less discussion than was necessary between HMI and their civil servant colleagues at the DES. *A Framework for the School Curriculum* (DES, 1980a) was produced without being influenced by HMI theoretical thinking on the curriculum contained in *Curriculum 11–16* (DES, 1977c). Within days of the publication of the DES *Framework*, HMI produced *A View of the Curriculum* (DES, 1980b), which continued their 'areas of experience' approach.

The HMI view of a common curriculum received a good deal of national support among teachers. *Curriculum 11–16* was not only a theoretical document, but a practical 'checklist' for LEAs and schools, and became the basis of a curriculum experiment for forty-one cooperating schools in five LEAs. This 'curricular reappraisal in action' led to two more influential HMI studies: *Curriculum 11–16: A Review of Progress* (DES, 1981b) and *Curriculum 11–16: Towards a Statement of Entitlement* (DES, 1983b). The 'areas of experience' approach to curriculum planning had been tried and found useful as a stimulus for school-based curricular rethinking. Thus HMI had not only developed a useful model for a broad and balanced curriculum, but had also engaged in its practical implementation in a number of schools. Yet this work was not always taken into consideration by the DES: as we shall see, when required to brief Ministers, DES civil servants tended to prefer the bureaucratic style of their own 1980–81 documents rather than the professionalism of HMI. The HMI initiative continued throughout the 1980s, however, with the *Curriculum Matters* series which extended the discussion of the whole curriculum from secondary schools to primary schools. Of particular importance was No. 2 in the series: *The Curriculum From 5 to 16* (DES, 1985b).

By this time, the curriculum had already become a party political issue. At the North of England Conference in January 1984, Sir Keith Joseph (now Lord Joseph) made three important announcements about future government policies: first, 'to define the objectives of the main parts of the 5 to 16 curriculum so that everyone knows the level of attainment that should be achieved...'; second, 'to alter the 16+ examinations so that they measure absolute, rather than relative performance'; third, 'to establish... the aim of bringing 80–90 per cent of all pupils at least the level which is now expected and achieved in the 16+ examinations by pupils of average ability in individual subjects; and to do so over a broad range of skills and competences in a number of subjects'. The Secretary of State also outlined four 'principles' to be observed in planning curricula: breadth, relevance, differentiation and balance.

At this time the strength of Sir Keith Joseph's position was that it combined the views of the three major power groups within the DES: the politicians, the bureaucrats and the professional HMI. The politicians wanted to control the curriculum, partly because some aspects of curriculum content were seen to be causing political concern; the DES civil servants wanted control as part of their new-found interest in policy, efficiency and value for money; HMI now had a professional interest in improving the quality of curriculum, felt that they had a means of achieving this, and saw it as part of their professional HMI role (Lawton and Gordon, 1987). The text of the speech by Sir Keith Joseph in 1984 shows evidence of all three influences: the language used is a mixture of the political, the bureaucratic and the professional.

One of the casualties of this 'united front' within the DES was the Schools Council. The Council had been in some disarray since the 1976 attack in the Yellow Book. An internal review had dutifully been carried out at the behest of the DES, and the constitution and structure of the Schools Council were revised in line with DES wishes. Nevertheless, in March 1981 the Secretary of State announced that Mrs Trenaman would review the work of the Council and make recommendations. Her report in October 1981 made some criticisms but recommended that the Schools Council should continue to exist and should not be subject to further review for the next five years. Notwithstanding this advice, in April 1982 the Secretary of State announced his intention to disband the Council in 1984. It was replaced by two separate bodies: a Secondary Examinations Council (SEC) and a Schools Curriculum Development Committee (SCDC) all of whose members would be appointed by the Secretary of State. The teachers' control of the curriculum was virtually over.

Meanwhile, Sir Keith Joseph's 1984 speech was being developed into an important policy document. It was published as a White Paper *Better Schools* (DES, 1985a). It contained an interesting revival of the statement of aims previously listed in *The School Curriculum* (DES, 1981c), with only minor changes in wording:

1   To help pupils to develop lively, enquiring minds, the ability to question and argue rationally and to apply themselves to tasks and physical skills.
2   To help pupils to acquire understanding, knowledge and skills relevant to adult life and employment in a fast-changing world.
3   To help pupils to use language and number effectively.
4   To help pupils to develop personal moral values, respect for religious values, and tolerance of other races, religions and ways of life.
5   To help pupils to understand the world in which they live, and the inter-dependence of individuals, groups and nations.
6   To help pupils to appreciate human achievements and aspirations.

This list of aims had been attacked by John White (1981) as an incoherent list which lacked priority and left open the question about the kind of educated person presupposed by these general expressions. It was, however, defended by a more sympathetic curriculum expert, Malcolm Skilbeck (1984), on the grounds that it was wrong to look upon policy statements as if they were educational treatises ...

'They often make points of a rhetorical kind, use language which refers to a current political position, and have to try to reconcile or hold together in a single document diverse and perhaps conflicting views on matters of current concern. This does not condone confusion or incoherence, but it does mean that we need not be unduly concerned about some roughness at the edges...' This was as true in 1985 as it had been in 1981. *Better Schools* gives a good deal of sensible advice about primary and secondary curricula, but in other places it is reminiscent of some of the earlier political concerns of Sir Keith Joseph and others on the right wing of the Party, for example, one of the concessions to the political right was the recommendation that 'the government believes that to assign a special place in the timetable to courses labelled "peace studies" unbalances the curriculum and over-simplifies the issues involved'.

Better Schools was addressed to LEAs and schools. The responses of LEAs to earlier Circulars on the curriculum (14/77, 6/81 and 8/83) were still not regarded as satisfactory. *Better Schools* can be seen as yet another attempt to prod LEAs into action. Three years after Circular 8/83 *The School Curriculum*, the DES produced the report *Local Authority Policies for the School Curriculum* (DES, 1986) which concluded with an interesting reference to future requirements:

> Progress in defining and applying nationally agreed objectives can only be made as a joint activity involving all the partners in the education service and the clients they serve.

A return to partnership, maybe, but not the kind of partnership which had existed in the 1950s and 1960s. LEAs and teachers were now clearly cast as junior partners required to follow directions from the centre.

In November 1986 a new Education Bill received Royal Assent. The 1986 Act was not essentially concerned with the curriculum but with the organisation of schools – in particular the role of parents and the functions of governing bodies. One of the results was, however, to give governors, including parent governors, more rights concerning the curriculum. The 1986 Act seems puny compared with the 1988 Act, but it was, nonetheless, of some importance in the move towards a national curriculum. Without a national curriculum the powers given to governors might have resulted in chaos.

Sir Keith Joseph resigned as Secretary of State for Education in 1986, and moved to the House of Lords, where he was to be an occasional critic of his successor, Mr Kenneth Baker. Joseph's sincerity was rarely questioned, but his views on education were clouded by his desire to reduce public expenditure, and it is very doubtful whether he could have implemented an effective national curriculum.

1987 was a busy year for the new Secretary of State, Mr Baker. In January he made a very important speech at Rotherham for the North of England Conference. He began by mentioning England's 'eccentric' education system – less centralised and standardised than, for example, France or Germany. He argued that existing standards were not high enough, and complained about the lack of agreement on the curriculum for the 14–16 age group, stressing the confusion in schools over the question of balance, and the failure to work out satisfactory objectives. He claimed that those weaknesses did not exist in those West European countries where the schools followed 'more or less standard national syllabuses'. Later in January the Secretary of State made a speech to the Society of Education Officers, explaining his ideas on a national curriculum to those who would be responsible for its implementation. In April, he outlined his proposals to the Education, Science and Arts Committee of the House of Commons.

An election was planned for 1987, and the Conservative Manifesto, published in May 1987, gave fair warning of 'the next moves forward'. Of the four major reforms in education, a national core curriculum was the first:

> It is vital to ensure that all pupils between the ages of 5 to 16 [sic] study a basic range of subjects – including maths, English and science. In each of these basic subjects syllabuses will be published and attainment levels set so that the progress of pupils can be assessed at around ages 7, 11 and 14, and in preparation for the GCSE at 16. Parents, teachers and pupils will then know how well each child is doing. We will consult widely among those concerned in establishing the curriculum.

After the June election, education was rarely out of the news, and progress towards 'the Great Education Reform Bill' was rapid. The Consultation Document on *The National Curriculum 5–16* was published in July 1987, and in September 1987 Mr Baker made a speech in Manchester elaborating on some of the proposals and answering some criticisms. The Consultation Document, which contained all the major aspects of the national curriculum enshrined in the Bill, will be discussed in Chapter 6. The Education Act 1988 received Royal Assent on 28 July.

SUMMARY

At the time of the 1944 Education Act, there would have been little support for the idea of a national curriculum, and there is no mention of curriculum in the 1944 Act. This vacuum led to the doctrine of teacher autonomy in curriculum matters – a doctrine which influenced the work of the Schools Council 1964–84. From 1960 onwards a number of social and political changes took place which made a national curriculum of some kind likely, whatever political party was in power. Those social pressures included:

1 Consumerism in education, and in particular the desire of parents to be well-informed and possibly to be involved in some aspects of curriculum decision making.
2 Pressure on the DES to control education (as well as to resource it) and to run an efficient, value-for-money system.

3   The curriculum became a (party) political concern for at least three reasons – populist appeal, a genuine concern to raise standards, and the realisation that the curriculum was potentially 'political' and might need to be controlled (especially when in the 'wrong' LEA hands).

Thus, the statement in the 1987 Conservative Manifesto (quoted on p.40) was 'acceptable' whereas ten or fifteen years earlier it would have been regarded as impossible.

THE 1988 EDUCATION ACT AND THE NATIONAL 6 CURRICULUM

The 1988 Education Act is a massive piece of legislation: with 238 clauses and 13 schedules, it is much more lengthy than the 1944 Act, and took more than 360 hours of parliamentary time, some of it in contentious debate in both Houses. It gave the Secretary of State 415 new powers, and provoked considerable opposition, partly because it represented a major shift of power in education to the central authority.

Apart from the national curriculum, the Act is concerned with the creation of grant-maintained schools (enabling schools to 'opt out' of LEA control and have a direct relationship with the DES); parental choice, especially in the form of open enrolment for schools; local financial management of schools; the abolition of the Inner London Education Authority (ILEA); changes in the funding and control of higher education (including tenure of university academics); and a number of miscellaneous items such as outlawing bogus degrees. This chapter will be concerned only with those parts of the Act impinging on the national curriculum.

Chapter 5 indicated that a national curriculum of some kind would almost certainly have been on the agenda whatever political party had been in power in the late 1980s; but the kind of national curriculum proposed might well have been different, given other political circumstances. One purpose of this chapter will be to outline the national curriculum; another will be to examine it critically, and to see what alternative models might have been possible.

This chapter will be concerned with the national curriculum for England only. The national curriculum in Wales poses particular problems, especially those associated with the Welsh language, which will require separate treatment to deal adequately with that issue.

There are many arguments in favour of the principle of a national curriculum. First, for example, it has been asserted, by HMI and others, that all children should be considered to have a right of access to a worthwhile curriculum (an entitlement curriculum); second, that there should be as much consensus as possible on the general aims and objectives of compulsory schooling; third, an egalitarian view, stressing equality of access to educational chances on a national basis, minimising local differences in the quality of education offered; fourth, that common schools should transmit a common culture by means of a common curriculum; fifth, that it is important for all schools to share common standards which would ensure reasonable levels of teacher expectation; sixth, that a national curriculum facilitates the geographical mobility of pupils; and seventh, that a national curriculum increases the accountability of schools and teachers.

Not all of the above arguments were advanced in favour of the Baker national curriculum – the final three were stressed, but passing references were made to some others, including the third. The kind of national curriculum proposed is necessarily associated with the arguments put forward in justification of a common or national curriculum.

The major arguments for the national curriculum are contained in the Consultation Document published in July 1987 *(The National Curriculum 5–16,* DES, 1987a). One of the complaints about this document was that whilst it claimed to be a 'consultation' opportunity, responses were required not later than the end of September; teachers organisations, LEAs and others complained bitterly about the lack of time given to prepare an adequate response. However, there were very strong political pressures on the DES officials to make rapid progress. Attempts were made to reassure teachers and others that this centralising measure would be an improvement:

> The government has concluded that these advantages and consistent improve-ments in standards can be guaranteed only within a national framework for the secular curriculum. To be effective, that must be backed by law – but law which provides a framework not a straitjacket. Legislation alone will not raise standards. The imaginative application of professional skills at all levels of the education service, within a statutory framework which sets clear objectives, *will* raise standards. (DES 1987a, para. 10)

The proposals for the national curriculum consisted of four components:

1 Foundation subjects
2 Attainment targets
3 Programmes of study
4 Assessment

FOUNDATION SUBJECTS

Within the list of foundation subjects, mathematics, English and science form the *core* of the curriculum – to be given first priority. Foundation subjects are to be followed by all pupils for the full length of compulsory schooling, that is, to age 16, except that a modern foreign language would not be included for primary schools. The majority of curriculum time at primary level should be devoted to the core subjects.

During the later years of secondary schooling, the suggested distribution of time for foundation subjects is as follows:

Foundation Subjects	%
English	10
Mathematics	10
Combined Sciences	10–20
Technology	10
Modern Foreign Language	10
History/Geography	10
Art/Music/Drama/Design	10
Physical Education	5

However, it is not the intention to allocate time for each subject area. It was suggested that foundation subjects 'commonly take up 80–90 per cent of the curriculum in schools where there is good practice'. A minimum of 70 per cent has sometimes been quoted. The rest of the time would be available for religious education and other subjects and areas.

In addition, there are a number of subjects or themes such as health education and use of information technology, which can be taught through other subjects. For example, biology can contribute to learning about health education, and the health theme will give an added dimension to teaching about biology. It is proposed that such subjects or themes should be taught through the foundation subjects, so that they can be accommodated within the curriculum but without crowding out the essential subjects. (DES 1987a, para. 18)

It will be necessary to return to critical comments on this aspect of the national curriculum later in the chapter.

ATTAINMENT TARGETS

Attainment targets will be set as soon as possible for the three core subjects.

These will establish what children should normally be expected to know, understand and be able to do at around the ages of 7, 11, 14 and 16, and will enable the progress of each child to be measured against established national standards... The range of attainment targets should cater for the full ability range and be sufficiently challenging *at all levels* to raise expectations, particularly of pupils of middling achievement who frequently are not challenged enough, as well as stretching and stimulating the most able. Targets must be sufficiently specific for pupils, teachers, parents and others to have a clear idea of what is expected, and to provide a sound basis for assessment. (Para. 23)

Other foundation subjects might have attainment targets 'where appropriate' but art, music and physical education would have guidelines rather than specific attainment targets.

PROGRAMMES OF STUDY

Subject working groups were set up in 1987 for mathematics and science and in 1988 for English and technology. The programmes of study were to be based on recommendations from the subject working groups. The programmes of study would be designed to reflect the attainment targets, and set out the overall content, knowledge, skills and processes which pupils should be taught, specifying in detail a minimum of common content which all pupils should be taught.

> Within the programmes of study teachers will be free to determine the detail of what should be taught in order to ensure that pupils achieve appropriate levels of attainment. How teaching is organised and the teaching approaches used will be also for schools to determine... Legislation should leave full scope for professional judgement and for schools to organise how the curriculum is delivered... (Para. 27)

ASSESSMENT

The attainment targets provide standards against which pupils' progress and performance can be assessed. Much of the assessment is intended to be done by teachers as an integral part of normal classroom work. The detailed scheme of assessment was entrusted to an expert Task Group on Assessment and Testing (TGAT) under the chairmanship of Professor Paul Black. (The TGAT Reports will be considered separately in Chapter 7.)

A controversial aspect of the assessment procedures was the stipulation that the results of assessment should be made publicly available. This requirement poses great difficulties both for those devising an assessment programme and for individual schools and LEAs responsible for the publication of results. During the consultation period much disquiet was expressed over the undesirable effects of 'league tables' of school results being made available without adequate explanation of background factors.

The Consultation Document (1987) and the Education Act (1988) provided for the creation of two new Councils: a National Curriculum Council (NCC) and a School Examinations and Assessment Council (SEAC). The NCC, replacing the School Curriculum Development Committee (SCDC), would be responsible for advising the Secretary of State on the national curriculum; all members of the council would be appointed by the Secretary of State. The NCC would have the task of keeping the national curriculum up to date, including amending attainment targets and programmes of study for foundation subjects. SEAC, replacing the Secondary Examinations Council (SEC), would be responsible for advice on qualifications offered during compulsory schooling (all of which would now be only permitted subject to approval by the Secretary of State), approving syllabuses and examinations leading to public qualifications, procedures for moderating standards of assessment at 7, 11, 14 and 16, and giving advice on criteria governing syllabuses and examinations and other kinds of assessment.

CRITICISMS OF THE NATIONAL CURRICULUM

A number of critics were disturbed by the bureaucratic style of the national curriculum documents which seemed to be more concerned with control than with improving quality; this was also associated with the fact that the Act gave the Secretary of State so many additional powers. Another criticism focused on the publication of test results, and connected publication with introducing market choice into educational planning. Above all, the national curriculum was condemned for being very old-fashioned: the subject basis of the curriculum ignored much of the curriculum thinking of the last twenty years (including the publications of HMI), and neglected important areas of learning such as political understanding, economic awareness, moral development, and many other cross-curricular themes. A final criticism was that the national curriculum was not truly national because it did *not* apply to independent schools: the Secretary of State was challenged on this issue in the House of Commons but refused to impose the national curriculum on the private sector.

Given the existence of much public and professional support for the principle of a national curriculum, why did Mr Baker choose such an unsatisfactory model? Since the discussions of the school curriculum during the 1970s (especially the Great Debate and after), it has been possible to identify two kinds of attitude towards the education system in England – the bureaucratic and the professional. Bureaucrats are necessarily concerned with the efficiency of the education service and need statistical information to demonstrate that efficiency. Professionals, however, are more concerned with the quality of the teaching process and the needs of individual children. The bureaucratic approach concentrates on output and testing, whereas the professional focuses on the quality of input and the responsibilities of the teacher. The bureaucratic approach is associated with norms, benchmarks, average performance and normative data, whereas the professional approach concentrates on individual differences, the learning process and criterion referencing. The bureaucratic curriculum will be based on traditional subjects; the professional regards subjects as a means of achieving higher level aims.

It is, however, important to stress that contrasting the two sets of attitudes in this way is not to regard them as a conflict between good and bad: civil servants have a perfectly legitimate concern for efficiency – it is part of their duty to ensure 'value for money' by means of accountability processes. It is also necessary to avoid the assumption that all civil servants are 'bureaucratic' in their attitudes to education; one of the right-wing complaints about the DES is that civil servants are part of the 'educational establishment', and even Conservative politicians have been accused of 'going native' in the DES, or being convinced by the 'professional' arguments of HMI. But it is, of course, possible to become too concerned with efficiency and to lose sight of the real purpose of the enterprise. If bureaucrats win too much influence at the expense of professionalism, there may be a danger of curriculum distortion. That is likely to happen at times when bureaucrats and the politicians in power share certain short-term objectives. The tension system within the DES is not a simple struggle between professionals and bureaucrats, but a three-way power game in which politicians sometimes have the deciding influence. There will be occasions when the dominant political concerns encourage bureaucrats to see education in an over-simplified way.

I have elsewhere suggested (1988) that it is useful to categorise political views on education into four ideological positions:

1 Privatisers
2 Minimalists or segregators
3 Pluralists
4 Comprehensive planners

One of the claims of modern Conservatism is that it is free from doctrine or ideology. The truth is that thinking within the Conservative Party comes from several different political traditions, sometimes representing contradictory sets of social attitudes and values; it is, therefore, more convenient to present the modern Conservative Party as completely pragmatic and eclectic. At least three of these four ideologies can be found within the ruling Conservative Party.

PRIVATISERS

Paradoxically, a very powerful tradition within the Conservative Party is nineteenth-century classical liberalism; those professing this political philosophy were suspicious of 'the state', objected to government interference in the private lives of citizens, including the idea of state schooling, and prefered a policy of intervening (and spending money) only in essential areas such as providing for national defence and a system of internal law and order. This 'libertarian' political philosophy is today often associated with economic monetarism – especially with views about keeping down public expenditure. Spending state money on many aspects of welfare is not only condemned for moral reasons as 'collectivism', it is also regarded as disastrous from an economic point of view. Politicians possessing those values and beliefs in a fairly extreme form would advocate the dismantling of the whole state education service or gradually privatising the system. I refer to this small, but vocal group, as the privatisers. For example, on 6 August 1987, Sir Alfred Sherman, formerly an adviser to the Conservative Party and still reputedly close to the Prime Minister, wrote in the *Daily Telegraph* advocating the privatisation of all schools ('How Everyone Could Have a Public School Education'). The fact that this group is most unlikely to succeed in achieving complete privatisation within education should not cause us to under-estimate their influence in moving educational policy in a right-wing direction. For example, Oliver Letwin, political adviser to Sir Keith Joseph on education and later to the Prime Minister, and still influential on the right-wing of the Party through the various pressure groups that exist, produced a book in 1988 interestingly entitled *Privatising the World*.

Throughout 1987 and 1988 right-wing groups such as the Hillgate Group were busy criticising some aspects of the Education Bill and denouncing HMI and others of the 'educational establishment' for their collectivist tendencies. Such groups would not, of course, be in favour of any kind of national curriculum, preferring to leave everything to market forces. On 19 November 1987, for example, Stuart Sexton, Director of the Education Unit of the right-wing Institute of Economic Affairs, wrote a letter to *The Independent* making two major criticisms of the Bill, one of which concerned the national curriculum:

The other mistake is over the national curriculum which is not a natural development from earlier Conservative policies and enactments. National curriculum proposals are really old hat, going back at least to the 1960s, dusted down off the shelf for each successive Secretary of State to consider. The nearest we need to a national curriculum was (sic) the reassertion of the three Rs on behalf of parents, which was inherent in Sir Keith Joseph's paper *Better Schools*.

The best 'national curriculum' is that resulting from the exercise of true parental choice by parents and children acting collectively, and being provided collectively by governors and teachers in response to that choice. The substitution for that freely adopted curriculum, geared to the needs of the particular children in question, of a Government-imposed curriculum is a poor second best. *(The Independent, 19 November 1987)*

As well as exerting a powerful constraining influence on curriculum policies, right-wing pressure groups were influential on other aspects of the legislation, giving full support, for example, to 'opting out' provisions and other 'market' features, as a step in the direction of full privatisation.

Privatisers once in office may be persuaded to adopt a more politically acceptable stance. For example, before becoming Secretary of State for Education, Sir Keith Joseph had been an outspoken critic of government interference in the market:

> The blind, unplanned, uncoordinated wisdom of the market... is overwhelmingly superior to the well-researched, rational, systematic, well meaning, cooperative, science-based, forward-looking, statistically respectable plans of governments... The market system is the greatest generator of national wealth known to mankind: coordinating and fulfilling the diverse needs of countless individuals in a way which no human mind or minds could ever comprehend, without coercion, without direction, without bureaucratic interference. (Joseph, 1976 in George and Wilding, 1985)

When he became Secretary of State for Education, Sir Keith Joseph could not publicly advocate privatisation as government policy; but he could deprive the state system of adequate funding.

Minimalists

Another powerful tradition within modern Conservatism is 'Tory paternalism' – the idea that God-given wealth and privilege bring with them duties and responsibilities towards the poor and the less favoured in society. In the nineteenth century such Conservatives tended to favour a state system of education, provided that it was not too costly and was not so good that it would challenge the privileges bestowed by private education. This tradition has continued into the twentieth century as a set of values supporting the provision of a state education system provided that value for money can be demonstrated, and also that education can be shown to be 'useful' particularly in the sense of servicing the labour market with well-trained and disciplined school-leavers who have been convinced of the value of such virtues as punctuality and hard work.

I have referred to this group of politicians as the minimalists. They support a state education service which concentrates on the basics, and their view of a national curriculum would emphasise a core of mathematics, English and other useful subjects. They would be suspicious of frills such as art and music, and hostile to political and economic awareness seeing them as potentially subversive.

Parents would have the right of buying additional extras or opting out altogether. Tawney criticised this attitude for producing a system run by those who felt that it was not good enough for their own children. Some voucher systems could operate within minimalism; the Assisted Places Scheme is typical of the belief that state schools are not really good enough for bright children; Mr Baker's City Technology Colleges are another example of minimalism.

PLURALISTS

There is yet a third group within the Conservative Party: those whose views occupy the middle ground in education and other aspects of welfare such as the Health Service. This group, sometimes referred to as the 'wets', are in the tradition of Butler in the 1960s, and in education, on the common ground established by Crosland in the Labour Party and Sir Edward Boyle, a Conservative Education Minister. This group of Conservatives, together with many in the Labour Party, would want a state system so good that there would be no incentive to use independent schools. Their regard for individual freedom of choice would not, however, allow them to legislate private schools out of existence. Freedom to choose is more important than social justice or equality of opportunity. Fabian socialists such as Crosland reluctantly came to this conclusion.

Pluralists invented terms such as 'parity of esteem' for the different, but equal, types of secondary school. They tend to hold meritocratic beliefs in education, favouring the metaphor of 'ladder of opportunity' rather than that of 'the broad highway'. In the past their view of the national curriculum was the now discredited 'core plus options' curriculum. Since his speech in the House of Commons in December 1987, Ted Heath has signalled his sympathy for this group. Similarly, moderate Conservative organisations such as the Conservative Education Association have much in common with pluralist views.

THE COMPREHENSIVE PLANNERS

'Comprehensive planners' is a useful term for those who recognise the necessity of changing the secondary curriculum to adjust to the needs of mass education. Comprehensive planners argue that a watered-down version of pseudo-high culture curricula will not do for a society committed to genuine secondary education for all. They also tend to criticise the grammar school curriculum for other reasons – epistemological, cultural and social as well as political (Lawton, 1983). Attempts to devise a common curriculum rest on ideological assumptions about common culture and common schools without denying individual differences and the need to provide for individual opportunities within a common plan. 'Common culture' is the key concept.

In 1973 I attempted to outline what would be a common curriculum, but not a uniform curriculum, with a strategy for planning a 'common culture individualised curriculum'. Such attempts to devise a common curriculum rest on ideological assumptions about common culture and common schools without denying individual differences and the need to provide for individual opportunities within a common plan. Comprehensive planners will generally tend to be in favour of centralised planning: Halsey (1983), for example, put forward a proposal involving

51

the possibility of LEAs being abolished; but they will also be concerned with the professionalism of teachers. For true comprehensive planners access must be completely open – the aim is a good general education for all ('the broad highway' metaphor). Excellence is defined in terms of enabling individuals to become autonomous learners; pupils should become successful self-educators across a wide range of cultural experiences.

If there are any comprehensive planners in the Conservative Party they have not been prominent in recent discussions on education.

The existence of the four ideologies, especially the first two, helps to explain why Mr Baker chose an obsolete, subject-based model, for planning his national curriculum. Politically he was under great pressure to move further in the direction of privatisation and minimalism; to have espoused the HMI 'areas of experience' curriculum model would have exposed him not only to a good deal of political criticism from the right-wing of his party, but also may have antagonised some senior civil servants, most of whom would be minimalists and pluralists suspicious of the non-subject curriculum model on grounds of lack of clear-cut accountability.

Thus the 1988 national curriculum is not a radical step forward; it is essentially backward-looking, and is seen as a virtue for that by many who would otherwise be doubtful about a national curriculum. The Baker national curriculum is a missed opportunity, but not, as some have suggested, a disaster. Much will depend on the quality of assessment procedures to be adopted. This aspect of national curriculum planning will be discussed in Chapter 7.

SUMMARY

The national curriculum is an important and highly controversial part of the 1988 Education Act. Some observers have been puzzled by this demonstration of centralist policy in a government which in other respects claims to be devoted to market forces and decentralisation. The Education Act, including the national curriculum, is, in effect, the result of a number of different, even contradictory, ideological pressures. The result is not a satisfactory or coherent policy on curriculum; but despite the degree of criticism occasioned by some aspects of the national curriculum, it is unlikely to work out as badly in practice as some have suggested. The national curriculum, if implemented in a sensible way by professional teachers, could be an improvement on the existing situation much criticised by HMI.

ASSESSMENT FOR THE
7 NATIONAL CURRICULUM

When details of the national curriculum proposal began to emerge during 1987, the aspect which caused most concern and critical comment was assessment at ages 7, 11, 14 and 16 – especially the danger of labelling children as failures at an early stage of their primary schooling. Since the publication of the Task Group on Assessment and Testing (TGAT) Reports, however, many teachers have been reassured, and some educationists now consider that the assessment procedures proposed by TGAT may represent the most positive features of the whole Act. Most of this chapter will be devoted to analysis of and comment on the TGAT Reports. They are important not only because they represent the most dramatic official curriculum innovation ever attempted in England, but also because they directly affect every primary and secondary school teacher.

The references to testing made in *The National Curriculum 5–16* raised objections of at least five kinds:

1 There was concern about the affect of testing on the pupils, especially what would happen to a child who 'failed' a test at age 7 or 11.
2 Testing would encourage teachers to concentrate on 'teaching to the test' rather than educating the children, with consequent narrowing and distortion of the curriculum.
3 Testing could adversely affect relations between parents and teachers.
4 The major reason for testing seemed to be to provide data so that 'league tables' of schools could be published for the 'market'.
5 There was an unresolved conflict between the kind of diagnostic assessment which many teachers welcomed and the normative testing needed for comparative purposes (and for league tables of good and bad schools).

TGAT was set up in July 1987, soon after the publication of the Consultation Document (DES, 1987a). The Group were given the very difficult challenge of devising a scheme of assessment by the end of the year. The First Report was produced on 24 December 1987 and published in January 1988; the three supplementary Reports followed at the end of March 1988. A helpful Digest of the First Report was also produced for discussion in schools (DES, 1988d).

A major achievement of the First Report was that it demonstrated to teachers and others that it was firmly embedded in sound curriculum principles. For example:

A school can function effectively only if it has adopted:

– clear aims and objectives;

– ways of gauging the achievement of these;
– comprehensible language for communicating the extent of those achievements to pupils, their parents and teachers and to the wider community, so that everyone involved can take informed decisions about future action.

Promoting children's learning is a principal aim of schools. Assessment lies at the heart of this process... (Para. 2 and 3)

It is also emphasised that assessment should be the servant, not the master, of the curriculum, and that it should also be an integral part of the educational process, providing 'feedback' and 'feedforward'. Four criteria are given priority:

1   Assessment results should be *criterion-referenced*.
2   They should be *formative*.
3   They should be calibrated or *moderated*.
4   Assessment should relate to *progression*.

The general approach which was adopted built on assessment procedures and practices already in existence, improving on them where necessary, and relating them to the specific new problems posed by the national curriculum. One general assumption made is that, far from distracting teachers from the teaching-learning process, good assessment helps teachers to know more about their pupils, and to teach more effectively. It is also pointed out that a good deal of testing (as well as assessment) already takes place in schools, including primary schools, but tends to be patchy in coverage, and it is of only local interest when what is required to complement a national curriculum, is a national system of assessment. However, no system yet exists anywhere in the world which entirely meets the four specified criteria: criterion-referenced, formative, moderated and involving progression.

The recommendations of the Task Group are intended to fit in with existing expertise and good practice: the assessments of individual children should continue to be the responsibility of teachers, and teachers' assessments should be a fundamental part of the new system. However, teachers will need more support, including a wider range of diagnostic tests for a minority of pupils. The TGAT proposals are mainly formative, providing information when deciding how pupils' learning may be taken forward. For 16-year-olds, the system is also *summative*, providing a comprehensive picture of the overall achievements of a pupil at the end of statutory schooling. At that stage, assessment will be linked with the General Certificate of Secondary Education (GCSE) grades.

In the Secretary of State's earlier utterances on the national curriculum and its assessment programme (quoted on p.45 of this book), a possible contradiction might be detected in that the national curriculum sets out what a pupil ought to know and understand at 7, 11, 14 and 16 'and will enable the progress of each child to be measured against established national standards'; but the statement goes on to say that 'the range of attainment targets should cater for the full ability range and be sufficiently challenging at all levels...'. During the early days of the discussion of the national curriculum in 1987, there were fears that, for example, nearly 50 per cent of 7-year-olds would be branded as failures by simple 'pass/fail' tests. This impression was encouraged by some on the right-wing of the Conservative Party like ex-Minister Sir Rhodes Boyson, who talked of additional vacation programmes for those who failed tests. Others appeared to be thinking along the lines of the continental practice of repeating a whole year's work if test results indicated sufficiently poor performance (ignoring the fact that the French have been trying very hard to eliminate this unsatisfactory practice of *redoublement* in their schools). TGAT had to try to meet the problem of assessing a curriculum which would have attainment targets, whilst avoiding rigid age-specific normative standards. This problem is discussed in *A Digest for Schools* (DES, 1988d):

The Group considered but rejected the idea of dividing children in each age group into five, or six or some other number of achievement levels that applied only to that age. In such a system, as the children move on from one reporting time to the next, neither they nor their parents are given a sense that they have made progress, although all should and virtually all do. In such a system, a child may start school life in the bottom grade and still be in it when he or she leaves.

Instead, the Task Group proposes that the reporting system should use a scale of 1 to 10 to cover the full range of progress that children of different abilities make between the ages of 5 and 16. Each number is to represent a level of achievement, so that level 1 is the first level in a profile component, no matter at what age that profile component is introduced. Many profiles components will have their origins before the reporting stage for 7-year-olds but, for example, the introduction of those for a modern foreign language will generally be after 11. A level should be so specified that it will represent the average educational progress of children over about two years. The sloping line in Figure 1 [Figure 2 in this book] represents this idea.

A pupil who has mastered the understanding and competence required for (say) level 1 will be working to achieve the criteria for level 2. Any one level, in this case level 2, represents the same competencies in the profile component no matter what the age of the child. In any one age group, some children will be at higher levels than others. The vertical broken lines on Figure 1 [2] represent this idea. *(A Digest for Schools, DES, 1988, p.8)*

The bold line gives the expected results for pupils at the ages specified. The dotted lines represent a rough speculation about the limits within which the great majority of pupils may be found to lie.

Thus a bridge is built between a curriculum which specifies achievement targets and an assessment system which must take into consideration different kinds of ability. The idea of ten levels has the advantage not only of avoiding the automatic linking of age to achievement, but also of building in progression for all pupils.

At age 7, only levels 1–3 will be used for most pupils. Achievement at level 1 for a 7-year-old will indicate that a child needs extra help to make satisfactory progress. On the other hand, achievement at level 3 will alert teachers to the need

Figure 2 *Sequence of Pupil Achievement of Levels Between ages 7 and 16*

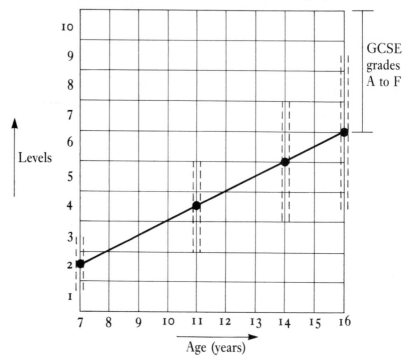

Source: *A Digest for Schools* (DES, 1988)

for special provision because the 7-year-old is moving ahead quickly. In both cases the children can be catered for within the class for their own age group. Nationally, the large majority of pupils will be at level 2; the use of levels 1 and 3 will probably occur more in some profile components such as reading than, for example, in art.

At age 11 nearly all pupils will be within levels 3, 4 and 5, but a small percentage may have reached level 6. It will be the teacher's responsibility to allocate levels, subject to moderation:

> During the year in which the pupils become 7, teachers would be asked:
> – on the basis of continuous assessment allied to programmes of study and attainment targets, to arrive at judgements of their pupils across a number of profile components and using three levels of performance;
> – to select from national item banks three standard tasks from within the range of work covered, at least one of which would be chosen in common with other local schools;
> – using the standard procedures and criteria for administration and for recording of performance, to incorporate the test tasks into their teaching programme so that each pupil is assessed, over three tasks, in the profile components;
> – to attend a local group moderation meeting at which they consider together

the results of the tests and their assessments, decide the overall distribution, resolve discrepancies and adjust individual levels in the light of the agreed distribution;
- to compile a confidential report for consideration by head and governors on the overall performance set against local and national distributions;
- to determine the levels for each pupil in the light of the profile components and of general information on standards as a whole, devised from the moderation meetings, and to report to parents;
- to enter results in the school records. (TGAT 1st Report para. 156)

For pupils aged 11, the same procedures would apply except that there would be three or four standardised assessment tasks (SATs) supplemented by external tests; the profile components would be more numerous and more complex; the information about school performance would be published; information on individual pupils would be made available to the secondary schools receiving them.

All of this not only gives a good deal of additional work to primary school teachers, especially at age 11, but also demands professional skills which may not yet be in evidence everywhere. The advantage of group moderation is that this process is itself an excellent method of in-service education for the teachers and helps in the development of professional assessment skills. (See Chapter 9 of this book.)

MODERATION PROCEDURES

Central to the procedures at 7, 11 and 14 is the principle of calibration or moderation (the third of the four high priority criteria). The process of moderation is discussed at some length in the First Report, and is usefully defined as 'bringing individual judgements into line with general standards'. Teachers are usually skilled at assessing their own pupils, but normally have no means of relating them to national standards. Another problem for teachers is the well-known 'halo' effect – the tendency to think that pupils 'good' in one area will be generally 'good'. A national system should help teachers to overcome these problems.

> All three statistical features of a set of school-based assessments – the mean, the spread and the rank order – are affected by fallibility in judgement, not because teachers are untrustworthy, but because they are human. The choice of a particular moderation method should recognise that distinction. (TGAT 1st Report para. 67)

The Report emphasises that moderation should *communicate* to teachers better ideas about general standards as well as *controlling* aberrations from standards by adjusting individual assessments. Three methods of moderation are discussed: scaling on a reference test, inspection by external moderators, and group moderation. Each method differs in its relative emphasis on *communication* or *control*.

A reference test is an external instrument set to the whole population of pupils being assessed by their teachers. Scaling assumes that performance on the test is a better guide to the average and spread of the performances in a class than the teacher's assessments. The teacher's marks are scaled accordingly. Standardised assessment tasks could be used in this way, but the simple ten level system (only some of which will be used in a class) makes adjustment of that kind very crude. Another disadvantage is that teaching might become dominated by tests.

Moderation by inspection avoids the above problem but still emphasises control rather than communication. It is also less effective than it looks because judgements are made by an external moderator on the basis of necessarily incomplete data.

Group moderation emphasises communication by means of exchange of samples at a meeting with other teachers. It is the approach used at GCSE, for example, or when examination boards scrutinise their own standards. Group moderation allows examiners to clarify the objectives and the bases of their own judgements. The Report claims that it 'is the only one of the three moderation methods which would enable the professional judgements of teachers to inform the development of the national curriculum'. (TGAT 1st Report para. 72)

When faced with a choice between high control and low communication, or high communication with less control, some bureaucrats and politicians might be expected to have a preference for control. At first, many educationists believed that the kind of assessment needed for the national curriculum would consist simply of batteries of standardised, pencil and paper, 'objective' tests for each subject. Teachers' assessments, if needed at all, would be controlled by the test results. It is a tribute to the quality of the writing in the TGAT Report that the DES civil servants, and later the politicians, were won over to the professional case, although it did provoke an argument between Mr Baker and the Prime Minister who, at least according to a leaked letter from her Private Secretary, though that the Group Moderation exercises would be unnecessarily complex and expensive. The arguments employed in the letter admirably represent right-wing attitudes to problems of professionalism and control:

From Paul Gray (Prime Minister's Private Secretary)
To Tom Baker (Secretary of State for Education's Private Secretary)

21st January 1988

Dear Tom

National Curriculum Task Group on Assessment and Testing Report

The Prime Minister has had the opportunity to look in more detail at this Report which your Secretary of State published last week. Although she agreed to your Secretary of State welcoming the Report as the broad framework into which attainment targets could be fitted, there are a number of aspects which she finds disturbing.

First, the Committee seem to have designed an enormously elaborate and complex system. They suggest it requires setting up *two* new powerful bodies, The Schools and Examinations Council (sic) and The National Curriculum Council, and a major new role for LEAs. Is this necessary? And has the sort of approach advocated in the Report in fact been put into practice with the proposed degree of elaboration in any large group of schools?

Second, the Prime Minister notes that the philosophy underlying the Report is that tests are only a part of assessment, and that the major purpose of assessment is diagnostic and formative rather than summative. As a result, the method of assessment places a heavy responsibility on teachers' judgements and general impressions. She is also concerned to note the major role envisaged for the LEAs in the implementation of the system.

Third, the Report does not pull together the overall costs of the exercise, but the general impression is that these would be very large. In view of the recommendation in Section XIX, the Prime Minister wonders whether, for example, the Group has considered the likely costs of training teachers prior to implementation and the regular annual costs of teachers' time once the system was in operation.

Fourth, the Prime Minister also notes that, presumably as a result of the complexity of the proposals, the new assessment system, could not be introduced in less than five years. Although she recognises the importance of careful preparation and introduction of the new arrangements, she is concerned that the process might take too long.

The Prime Minister would be grateful if your Secretary of State could take these concerns into account in his further considerations of the Report and the continuing dialogue with the Task Group.

I am copying this letter to the Private Secretaries to other members of E (EP).

Yours,
Paul Gray

(Published in *The Independent*, 10 March 1988)

A compromise was eventually reached: a shorter time for implementation has been accepted, and the extent to which teachers' judgements will be externally moderated has yet to be precisely determined. In practice, it has usually been found that when teachers are in doubt they tend to look for external standards to confirm or adjust their own judgements.

Part of the reason for the acceptance of the TGAT Report by the DES civil servants and politicians was the fact that it will 'deliver' the required bureaucratic data – that is, pupils' scores can be aggregated to show results for a class, a school and a whole LEA for comparative purposes. The TGAT recommendations, including the three Supplementary Reports, are essentially a compromise – giving civil servants and politicians the kind of information they need for accountability and control (and market choice) without sacrificing professional principles. League tables of schools will emerge, but it will be up to the professionalism of teachers and LEAs to put them into a meaningful context for public consumption. Some educationists may feel that the schooling system would be better without such 'league tables', but they have failed to persuade parents and politicians on that issue. The kind of consumerism fostered by current government policies includes 'the right to know' this kind of information. The art is to provide that information without damage to pupils, teachers and the quality of the teaching-learning process.

A very important principle is that assessment should be, as much as possible, an integral part of teaching:

> Provided the requirements of national comparability are met, the system we propose allows a degree of flexibility at the school level. For example, where provided externally, the particular test topics or themes may be a prescribed set, or an agency may provide a range from which schools can make their own choice. The form in which a task is administered may be prescribed, but it may not have to be done at fixed times – particularly for tests of a project nature which may extend over several class periods. If such flexibility is to be accommodated – which we think very desirable – then marking or grading procedures will have to be carefully standardised, and there will also have to be some means of moderation between teachers and schools.
>
> We recommend that the national system should employ tests for which a wide range of modes of presentation, operation and response should be used so that each may be valid in relation to the attainment targets assessed. These particular tests should be called 'standard assessment tasks' and they should be so designed that flexibility of form and use is allowed wherever this can be consistent with national comparability of results. (TGAT 1st Report para. 50)

Much has already been gained by secondary teachers in this respect by using course work as part of the overall assessment for GCSE; but primary schools are less accustomed to assessment of this kind. The Task Group were clearly aware of the problems and the advantages involved. The *Digest* suggests that fo 7-year-olds, assessment would take the form of topics designed to look like ordinary, interesting pieces of work. In the course of doing the work, 7-year-old pupils would display a range of achievements which teachers assess by observing children's activity and by marking work. 'The advantage of the approach is that children are much more likely to show what they can really do when they are involved in activities which for them are normal and have a clear purpose' (*Digest*, p.11–12). The Task Group recommended three tasks for 7-year-olds, and probably four for the 11-year-olds to allow for a greater number of profile components. For 11-year-olds, tasks may be supplemented by tests more specifically targeted on profile components for particular subject areas.

Defining the profile components will be the responsibility of the subject working groups set up by the Secretary of State. Within each subject there will be a small

Figure 3 *Evolution of profile components*

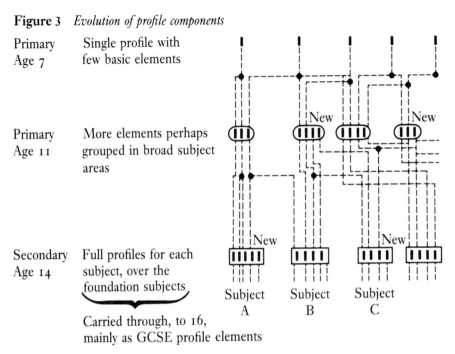

Primary Age 7	Single profile with few basic elements
Primary Age 11	More elements perhaps grouped in broad subject areas
Secondary Age 14	Full profiles for each subject, over the foundation subjects

Subject A   Subject B   Subject C

Carried through, to 16,
mainly as GCSE profile elements

Source: *A Digest for Schools* (DES, 1988)

number (preferably no more than four and never more than six) profile components reflecting the variety of knowledge, skills and understanding of the subject. (For example, within English the profile components might be reading, writing, listening and oral fluency.) Wherever possible, the Task Group recommends that one or more components should have more general application across the curriculum.

One advantage of this pattern of assessment is that it will encourage thinking about the curriculum as a whole, for example, considering what components various subjects might have in common. Another advantage is that some of the 'themes' or curriculum areas such as economic understanding, left out of the list of national curriculum subjects, can be reintroduced. This will be partly a task for the Secretary of State's subject working groups, and partly for schools themselves to work out in detail. At the time of writing this book, the subject working groups' final recommendations had not been published. Much will depend on the quality of their work; their responsibilities are considerable:

We recommend that each of the subject working groups define a sequence of levels in each of its profile components, related to broad criteria for progression in that component. For a profile component which applies over the full age range 7 to 16, there should be ten such levels, with corresponding reduction for profile components which will apply over a small span of school years. (TGAT 1st Report para. 101)

61

When tasks have been completed the process of moderating the results will begin. Teachers will then have two sets of information – their own assessments of each pupil's levels of attainment and marks arising from tasks or tests. At this stage teachers from a group of schools will attend a moderation meeting with examples of children's work. One function of the meeting will be to compare the spread of results, from all of the tasks or tests, with the spread of results from teachers' assessments. 'For example, for 7-year-olds, the teachers' assessments of a particular profile component may show that 10 per cent of children are at level one, 80 per cent at level 2, and 10 per cent at level 3. The results from the national assessment tasks may show virtually the same distribution, or they may be different, say 5 per cent, 75 per cent, 20 per cent. The moderating group will have to consider such discrepancies...' (*Digest*, p. 13). The moderating group will have to decide whether the assessment of those teachers should be rescaled; or whether local factors could justify rescaling the national results; or whether the national tests results are in need of adjustment. Results will be reported back via a regional agency to the School Examinations and Assessment Council (SEAC) which will decide whether the local action taken was appropriate.

REPORTING RESULTS

Assessment by teachers should be continuous, as should feedback to and discussion with pupils. The reporting years 7, 11 and 14 are times for checking standards with other schools and with national standards. The Task Group also mentions the use of Records of Achievement (which will be a requirement for all schools in 1990) as an important vehicle for recording pupils' progress in conjunction with formal reporting at 7, 11 and 14. Parents will continue to receive annual reports which could now be linked to national standards by referring to the ten levels of performance. Parents will also be given information about the proportion of children in the age group reaching the various levels (within the school and nationally) at 7, 11 and 14, as well as having access to the individual child's achievement which will, of course, be confidential. (Apart from being available to parents, they would only be made available to the school to which the pupil is transferring.) As well as using these formative tests, teachers will be encouraged to use appropriate diagnostic tests for some individual pupils, maybe in association with the LEA's educational psychologist.

On the occasion of the formal reporting times, a school will examine the spread of levels achieved in the various profile components and consider whether any internal action is necessary. At the same time, the LEA will be collecting and considering information about the spread of results for the schools. They may identify schools in need of support, taking into account the general circumstances of the school and the catchment area.

The results for each age group need careful interpretation. The Group proposes that they should be made available to enquirers, but *only as part of a more general statement about a school*, produced by the school and authenticated by the LEA. The LEA should also provide material, for inclusion in the statement, describing the influence of factors, such as the socio-economic nature of the catchment area on a school's results. (*Digest*, p. 16)

This form of assessment may also be of help to some children with special needs: their curriculum will be the same as others but the route towards it can be much more flexible within the TGAT scheme. However, Professor Klaus Wedell (1988) has expressed doubts about the national curriculum in the context of children with special educational needs.

THREE SUPPLEMENTARY REPORTS

The three Supplementary Reports, published as a single volume (DES, 1988c) dealt with the following issues:

First Supplementary Report: reactions to the main Report

This Report examined issues raised in reaction to the main Report and reaffirmed that a balance was required between standardised tests and other forms of assessment, and that the use of 'externally prescribed tests and of teachers' own assessments, combined through effective moderation procedures' would give the best means of securing standards, enhancing professional skills and improving learning. The Report warned that no alternative or simplified system could achieve what was needed.

Second Supplementary Report: application of the framework to individual subjects

This Report records discussions with subject specialists. General agreement was reached but close liaison will be needed in order to secure consistency in the definition of profile components and to ensure that elements common to two or more subjects are suitably reflected without omission or duplication. Subject working groups will need to pay attention to the balance of assessment in fields such as the arts; to give priority to developing descriptions of progression; to clarify attainment targets and profile components; to advise on aggregation of results; and to advise on in-service training needs.

Third Supplementary Report: A system of support

The Report recommends a structure involving a regional tier between national agencies and district level moderating groups. The regional tier would consist of up to twelve consortia formed by GCSE groups and LEAs. In-service training will be essential. The Report proposes an awareness programme for headteachers 1988–89. A case study showed how a typical LEA might redeploy existing resources in support of national curriculum and assessment. It is suggested that the process could be much less expensive than had been suggested in some quarters.

The three Supplementary Reports were welcomed by the Secretary of State, but the debate about the complexity of the procedures – and the costs – continued. By this time it seemed to be generally agreed that, as was stated in the First Supplementary Report, there was no alternative to the TGAT scheme if quality was the real objective. However, many details of procedures remain to be settled.

Summary

Many teachers are suspicious of 'external' assessment systems, especially in primary schools. One problem is that education is essentially concerned with long-term aims, whereas assessment has to deal with what can be observed now. The art of assessment is to reconcile that difficult gap as much as possible, by making assessment an integral part both of the long-term curriculum plan and of the day-to-day teaching process. This is an expert, professional matter and needs sensitivity towards teachers and their concerns. Professor Black and his colleagues on TGAT have planned an excellent outline scheme 5–16 incorporating the four priority criteria (criterion referencing, formative assessment, moderating and progression). The avoidance of a direct relation between age and achievement levels is perhaps the most promising innovation. Much of the detailed work has still be to completed, and a good deal will depend on the expertise and sensitivity of the subject working groups.

The second significant achievement of TGAT is that it has managed to bridge the gap between professional standards and bureaucratic needs (or, as stated in the Report, between communication and control). One of the problems in this area is that there are always easy solutions available, if control is the only consideration: testing agencies and publishing houses will always be ready to produce a neat, 'user-friendly' test for almost any purpose; but it may have little real connection with the complex plans of a long-term national curriculum. As those concerned with the Assessment of Performance Units (APU) discovered, many of the existing simple testing instruments give little, if any, useful information about pupils' educational achievements.

The third achievement of TGAT is that it starts from where teachers are and steers them in the direction of greater professionalism. The TGAT proposals present a tremendous challenge and opportunity to the teaching profession. In the course of meeting that challenge they will develop continuously as professionals. In the past, assessment and record-keeping have not been the strongest features in many primary and secondary schools; teachers will now have an opportunity to develop better procedures and also to demonstrate a wider repertoire of teaching techniques. They will, however, have to be very vigilant to avoid assessment becoming a meaningless bureaucratic exercise rather than an integral part of the teaching-learning process.

8 | CURRICULUM PLANNING AND EXAMINATIONS

The English are not generally thought of as great curriculum planners, but in many respects they have led the world in the field of examinations. They are good at organising public examinations, setting papers, insisting on fairness, and generally treating the examining process with great seriousness. David Lodge's fictional arch-examiner, Philip Swallow, was surely based on observations of reality, and such painstaking devotion to examining duties is widespread in secondary schools as well as in English universities:

> He was a superlative examiner of undergraduates: scrupulous, pain-staking, stern yet just. No one could award a delicate mark like B+/B+ ?+ with such confident aim, or justify it with such cogency and conviction. In the department meetings that discussed draft question papers he was much feared by his colleagues because of his keen eye for the ambiguous rubric, the repetition of questions from previous years' papers, the careless oversight that would allow candidates to duplicate material in two answers. His own papers were works of art on which he laboured with loving care for many hours, tinkering and polishing, weighing every word, deftly manipulating *eithers* and *ors*, judiciously balancing difficult questions on popular authors with easy questions on obscure ones, inviting candidates to consider, illustrate, comment on, analyse, respond to, make discriminating assessments of or (last resort) discuss brilliant epigrams of his own invention disguised as quotations from anonymous critics...
> (*Changing Places*, pp. 17–18: Penguin)

Public examinations for English schools date back to the mid-nineteenth century; the emphasis on external assessment is much more important than, for example, the Baccalaureat in France or the Abitur in Germany. The historical reasons for this will be set out below, and have a good deal to do with the desire to move away from eighteenth-century patronage to a fair competitive system – and fairness was ensured by an external objective assessment system. This had many advantages in the short run, but in the longer term caused certain distortions, and examinations sometimes seemed to become more important than education itself.

One of the problems for those who set up external public examinations is that on the one hand they want to control schools by means of the examination structure, but on the other hand, official bodies often bemoan the fact that examinations dominate the curriculum and prevent teachers from concentrating on education. So the Norwood Committee (1943), for example, wanted to move away from national control by giving teachers much greater local involvement. Since then almost every enquiry into secondary education has repeated the maxim that examinations should be the servant not the master of the curriculum (Mortimore *et al.*, 1986). However, in the absence of strong curriculum regulations or guidelines there will be a tendency for the examination syllabus to become the curriculum – providing the objectives, sequence and structure that would otherwise be lacking. Apart from the danger of the tail wagging the dog, we shall see that this kind of examination dominance has other serious disadvantages.

This chapter will consist of four overlapping sections: (*a*) a brief historical survey showing the development of examinations; (*b*) a closer look at examinations at age 16, particularly the new General Certificate of Secondary Education (GCSE); (*c*) the curriculum and examination problem 16–19, including GCE A levels, and AS levels; and (*d*) other school examinations and forms of assessment.

In each section the same themes will be seen to emerge: the tension between administrative control and teacher or school autonomy; the conflicting demands of the bureaucratic concern for efficiency and professional standards of quality. However, it would be a mistake to see the argument in a one-sided way. Anyone familiar with the history of schools in the nineteenth century, or even readers of Dickens' fictional accounts of school conditions, may have a sneaking feeling that greater control was overdue; and although greater teacher professionalism must be a goal for those involved in planning an improved educational system, it should not be seen as unbridled licence or complete independence from non-professional opinion.

EXAMINATIONS IN ENGLAND: HISTORICAL BACKGROUND

Public examinations as we know them today are very much a nineteenth-century creation. After the reforms of Oxford and Cambridge Universities and the passing of the Oxford Public Examinations Statute in 1800, written examinations became part of the system of assessment for final degrees. A little later some professional bodies introduced written papers as part of the set of qualifications necessary to become admitted to membership: for example, the Society of Apothecaries in 1815, and the Solicitors in 1835. In the 1840s HMI used written examinations to select elementary school teachers.

Perhaps of even greater significance were the Cardwell army reforms and the Northcote-Trevelyan reforms of the civil service: responding to demands for greater efficiency in the mid-nineteenth century, competitive examinations were introduced for entry to the military academies and to the various branches of the civil service. Some schools responded by setting up a 'Civil Service Class' specifically to prepare boys for these entrance examinations. Later, the London

Matriculation Examination was used to 'exempt' candidates from those more specific entrance tests.

It had also become customary for some schools anxious to demonstrate their efficiency to invite an independent assessor to inspect and report on their achievements. This 'examiner' was often a Fellow of one of the Oxford or Cambridge colleges. However, one disadvantage of this practice was the lack of comparability between schools, and the fact that those schools most needing inspection would avoid it. In 1857 the Bath and West of England Society for the Encouragement of Agriculture, Arts, Manufacture and Commerce set up a committee to organise an examination for local schools. This 'Exeter Experiment' paved the way for an annual examination validated by the Universities of Oxford and Cambridge. The 'Locals' began in 1858, and in 1877 Oxford began issuing certificates to successful candidates.

An even more influential development was the University of London Matriculation Examination. The London Matriculation had existed since 1838 but was mostly taken by those proceeding to a university degree; gradually its use was extended to an all-purpose School Leaving Examination recognised by employers as being of an appropriately high standard, so that by 1870 only half of the candidates were using the examination for the purpose of entry to university.

In 1903 the Senior School Certificate was established by the University of London as a more general leaving certificate (which later developed into the School Certificate). This examination structure had the effect of broadening the secondary school curriculum – English and science, for example, became required subjects. Other universities followed: in 1903 the northern universities, for example, formed their own Joint Matriculation Board (JMB). Increasingly, professional bodies used Matriculation examinations as qualifying tests rather than establish their own tests of admission.

From time to time it was suggested that there should be some kind of centralised system for school examinations; but Lingen, Secretary of the Education Committee, had refused to involve the central authority in 1857. There was still a good deal of hostility to the idea of state control, but not yet enough professional confidence to allow teachers themselves to take control. The Bryce Report 1895 recommended a central office for examinations, but after the Acts of 1899 and 1902 the new local education authorities preferred university control rather than increasing the power of the central authority. In 1904 the Board exerted its authority by forbidding external examinations during the first two years of secondary schooling, but still did not seek to establish direct control of examinations. Yet coordination of some kind was needed: in 1917 a compromise was found after consultations between the Board, the universities, and professional bodies. The Secondary School Examinations Council (SSEC) was set up to advise the Board; it consisted of twenty-one members – a balance of representatives from local authorities, the teachers and the universities. It began work by coordinating the new School Certificate and Higher School Certificate set by the separate universities. There were already complaints that schools were dominated by examinations, and also that public examinations were dominated by the   69 universities, so that the secondary school curriculum was being sacrificed to university entrance requirements (Spens Report, 1938).

During the 1920s and 1930s, the number of pupils taking School Certificate examinations increased, despite growing criticism of the examination structure. The School Certificate was unpopular with some teachers, and especially headteachers, because it was a group examination (a candidate had to pass at least five subjects, some of which were compulsory). Teachers complained that every year good pupils were denied a certificate. This was an excellent example of the danger of using an examination structure to enforce a 'broad curriculum'. It took a very long time for teachers and others to recognise the dangers of trying to use an examination as a method of curriculum control.

The Spens Committee was set up in 1933 to consider the provision of education for pupils beyond the age of 11. It had a good deal to say about the school curriculum, but not very much directly concerning examinations, except to lament the influence of the universities on the School Certificate in reinforcing a traditional academic pattern. The Report expressed confidence in the ability of the psychologists to select different types of children at 11+, and recommended separate technical schools and other kinds of secondary schools for the 85 per cent of the population for whom the grammar school curriculum would not be appropriate.

The discussion about curriculum and examinations at 16 was temporarily set aside with the onset of World War II, but as early as 1941 another Committee, chaired by Cyril Norwood, was appointed by the President of the Board of Education, R. A. Butler, to 'consider suggested changes in the Secondary School curriculum and the question of School Examinations in relation thereto'. The Norwood Report was much criticised but extremely influential: it accepted the 'psychological' notion of three kinds of pupil needing different kinds of curriculum, and provided a justification for the post-1944 tripartite arrangements for secondary schooling adopted by most LEAs. On the question of the School Certificate, Norwood criticised the existing examination structure because it dominated and distorted the curriculum.

> We believe that in the long run it is to the advantage of the secondary Grammar School and the education which it offers that there should be a new conception of the function of examinations at 16+, and a change in the nature of any School Certificate awarded at this stage. Examination plays a necessary part in the school economy... But it should be a subordinate part, and similarly in any certificate of performance the results of examination should be only one element in a comprehensive survey of the pupil's life at a secondary Grammar School. If this is the right place of examinations in school economy and in a school certificate, we think that ideally the examination is best conducted by the teachers themselves as being those who should know their pupils' work and ought therefore to be those best able to form a judgement on it.

This was regarded as a long-term goal; in the meantime three specific recommendations were made:

1 The School Certificate should continue to be run by university examining bodies.
2 Schools should offer their own syllabuses.
3 Examinations should be subject examinations, that is, without restrictions as to numbers of subjects or compulsory subjects.

In effect, Norwood was making a very radical suggestion: that assessment should be a combination of a written examination and what later became known as a record of achievement or profile.

Unfortunately, as so often happens with such reports, some of the recommendations were eventually implemented but not others. Thus, Norwood has sometimes been blamed for the imperfections of the GCE examination which replaced the School Certificate in 1951, but these imperfections would not have been so serious had the parallel suggestions about records of achievement been adopted at the same time.

In August 1947, the reconstituted SSEC reported their view on the Norwood proposals and unanimously recommended a single subject examination, but the new pass level for GCE O level was to be at the standard of a credit of the old School Certificate, rather than a simple pass. The single subject structure, however, removed the only support, albeit an unsatisfactory one, for a broad and balanced curriculum up to 16. From 1944 there were no regulations controlling the secondary curriculum; from 1951 there was no examination incentive for maintaining a broad and balanced curriculum.

EXAMINATIONS AT 16+: THE GCSE

When the GCE O level examination was established in 1951, it was designed for roughly the top 20 per cent of the 16-year-old population. The other 80 per cent were reckoned to be unexaminable, or more charitably, that they should be left free from the constraints of examinations. It was not long, however, before secondary modern schools responded to pressures from parents and employers by introducing a variety of external examinations for their more academic pupils. The situation was aggravated by the inadequacies of the selection processes which resulted in a not insignificant proportion of pupils being incorrectly placed in secondary modern schools. From the mid-1950s schools began to agitate for a national examination, and the Ministry of Education reacted to pressures by setting up a committee – the Beloe Committee – which reported in 1965. The Beloe Report recommended a single subject examination designed for the 40 per cent of boys and girls who, at 16, were below the top 20 per cent destined for O levels.

Almost as soon as this new examination – the Certificate of Secondary Education (CSE) – was established, many teachers felt that a single, common examination at 16+ would be better. In 1970 the Schools Council voted in favour of a common examination at 16+ and embarked upon an expensive programme of development and feasibility studies for a joint examination. This resulted in a Report (1975) in favour of a common examination. However, consideration of this Report unfortunately coincided with the growing criticism of the education service (including criticism of teachers) which provoked Callaghan's Ruskin Speech (1976) and subsequent moves by the DES towards greater centralisation. There was an inevitable clash between the idea of greater teacher control of the examination at 16+, and the desire by the DES for greater central control of the curriculum. Thus, Shirley Williams, the Labour Secretary of State for Education, instead of accepting the Schools Council recommendation for a single 16+ examination, yielded to civil service pressure to set up yet another committee to look into the problem. The Waddell Committee reported in 1978 (DES, 1978c) recommending a single system of examining at 16+, but this had not only delayed the implementation of the examination by several years, but had also introduced the idea of differentiated papers, which some have claimed negates the main purpose of a common examination (Gipps, 1986).

There was, however, still much ground to be covered before the common 16+ examination began: a White Paper *Secondary School Examinations: A Single System at 16+* (DES 1978d) was published, but in the following year any further progress was blocked by the change in government. The 1979 Conservative administration was predictably less favourably disposed towards a common examination, and successive Conservative Secretaries of State gave increasing emphasis to the notion of differentiation and differentiated papers within what was now referred to as a common *system* of examinations at 16+. An even more interesting development was the insistence by the Secretary of State for Education on the establishment of 'national criteria' for subjects to be offered in the new examination. In 1977 the House of Commons Expenditure Committee (10th Report) had called for greater comparability between the Boards, and this was taken up again by the Waddell Report (DES, 1979c) in the form of a suggestion that there should be national criteria. The Government's acceptance of the Waddell recommendations in 1980 included a specific commitment to national criteria. It is doubtful whether national criteria will produce greater comparability between Boards, but their existence certainly provide scope for much stronger central control.

GCSE national criteria

From 1980 onwards a good deal of time and energy has been devoted to national criteria. The GCE and CSE Boards were invited to draft the criteria for twenty of the most important subjects. They formed a Joint Council, largely for this purpose, which has, since the establishment of GCSE, found a continued existence and identity of its own. Working Parties were set up for the twenty subject areas, and they were charged with the task of producing agreement on: the title; the general aims of the syllabus; the assessment objectives (together with the proportion of marks to be awarded for each assessment objective); the scheme of assessment, including details of examination *components* (an important new term); and explanation of how differentiation would be achieved; descriptions of the standards of grades C and F – C being the lower end of the old GCE 'pass', F being the equivalent of CSE Grade 4 (the 'average' candidate). The full range of equivalences is shown as follows:

GCE	CSE	GCSE
A		A
B		B
C	1	C
	2	D
	3	E
	4	F
	5	G
	U	U

Some of the twenty Working Parties took the opportunity to examine the nature of their subject and what the knowledge, skills and understanding within it might offer to the curriculum as a whole. In some cases the result was a considerably different 'subject' from the old GCE version; one of the problems for the future was the diminished continuity between the 16+ examination and GCE A level.

In 1984 completed sets of draft criteria were sent to the DES for approval; but by then the Secretary of State for Education, Keith Joseph, had changed the rules in an interesting way. In his famous Sheffield speech (January 1984), Sir Joseph put on record his conviction that standards should be raised and that he saw the 16+ examination as one important means of achieving this. He envisaged two kinds of change: a larger proportion of 16-year-olds achieving higher grades (at least 80–90 per cent reaching the level currently associated with average performance – i.e. CSE Grade 4); and a move towards 'absolute standards' rather than statistically adjustable results – criterion-referenced rather than norm-referenced grades. The Secondary Examinations Council (SEC), which had taken over examination responsibilities from the Schools Council, was given the task of establishing eighteen Working Parties, this time to produce national *grade criteria*.

GCSE 1988

Fortunately the implementation of GCSE was not delayed until the national grade criteria were established – it soon became clear that this was a very difficult, if not an impossible exercise. (See Kingdon and Stobart, 1988 for a description of these problems.) The final versions of the national criteria, together with a document on

73

general criteria, were published in March 1985; it was also announced that the first examination would take place in the Summer of 1988 (teaching beginning in September 1986 – too little planning and preparation time, the teachers and Examination Boards complained).

From 1986 to 1988 teachers continued to complain about lack of adequate preparation and training, and some syllabuses and other materials reached schools late, but the first examination took place in June 1988 without any major disasters. HMI had monitored the teaching for GCSE and came to the conclusion that the new style of examination had raised standards and improved the quality of teaching, despite the fact that the in-service training, conducted on a 'cascade' basis, was generally considered to be far from adequate. The idea of an examination based on 'positive achievement' of what pupils 'knew, understood and could do' had much to be said for it; the other successful feature was teacher-assessed course work: although there were some complaints by both teachers and pupils about the workload involved, in general this feature of the new GCSE was considered to have contributed to its success.

CURRICULUM AND EXAMINATIONS 16–19

There are two main problems for schools at the post-16 level: first, GCE A level is far too specialised and lacking in balance, even for academic 18-year-olds; second, there has been a healthy increase in the number of boys and girls staying on after age 16, for many of whom the A level course is unsuitable. Over the years several solutions have been suggested for both problems, but a complete answer has not yet been found.

Attempts to reform GCE A level

The A level problem is another example of using an examination as a curriculum rather than as a means of evaluating a curriculum. Historically the A level examination evolved out of the Higher School Certificate/ Intermediate degree examinations – i.e. a stage between Matriculation (which was intended to be evidence of a broad general education) and first degree finals examinations which would be more specialised. Specialising in two or three subjects as an early stage of a degree course might be acceptable, but to have the same curriculum for young people aged 16–18 whether or not they are proceeding to higher education is even more questionable.

In 1959 the Crowther Report referred to the highly specialised sixth form curriculum but did not recommend any change:

> In England it [i.e. specialisation] begins... earlier than in any other country. From the age of 15, or 16 at latest, the classical specialist in an English school

will spend only a small part of his actual school time on anything but Latin, Greek and ancient history; the equivalent is true of the mathematician or scientist. (*Crowther Report*, 1959)

Others were, however, much more critical and saw the need for a more balanced and broad curriculum 16–19. In 1961, 360 headteachers of schools with sixth forms signed an Agreement to Broaden the Curriculum (ABC) pledging themselves to devote one-third of the sixth form timetable to non-specialist work. In 1962, the General Studies Association was founded with similar aims. However, these were essentially attempts to patch up a curriculum structure which was seriously defective, and the power of the examination proved too great for these well-meaning expressions of intent.

When the Schools Council was established in 1964, the 16–18 curriculum was one of its areas of priority, but throughout its twenty years' existence the Schools Council was unable to produce a reform which was acceptable to all – especially to the universities who, whilst paying lip-service to general education, had grown accustomed to receiving 18-year-olds as undergraduates who had already covered some of the ground necessary for a degree programme. Universities tended to speak with two voices: one, a genuine concern for general, liberal education, expressed by Vice-Chancellors and others; two, a more parochial insistence, by admissions tutors, on 'standards' of specialised knowledge for those who wished to embark upon a first degree programme. Thus it was not totally unreasonable for the universities to be party to a joint statement with the Schools Council in favour of a broader curriculum (in 1966) but to reject specific proposals a few years later.

Schools Council Working Paper No.5 (1966) suggested that able sixth formers should study two major and two minor subjects (instead of two or three A levels); less-academic pupils might take more minor courses but fewer majors; all would take General Studies. In March 1968 a Joint Working Party of the Schools Council and the Standing Committee on University Entrance (SCUE) was set up which produced proposals for two levels of sixth form study – Q and F. A broad education was to be achieved by changing university entrance requirements to five subjects at 'qualifying level' (Q) after one year in the sixth form, and up to three subjects at the end of the second year (F). These proposals were much discussed but eventually rejected, partly on the grounds of the undesirability of young people having to do a public examination at ages 16, 17 and 18.

The Joint Schools Council/SCUE Working Party next proposed a five subject curriculum, examined at two levels in the same year: three N (normal) and two F (further) level examinations; N would be roughly half the work of an A level, and F would be three quarters – three N + two F being theoretically no more work than three A levels. In 1974 the Schools Council set up feasibility studies and fifty-six groups set to work producing N and F syllabuses with specimen examination papers. Results were reported in December 1976, and more detailed studies began in 1977. However, as we have seen in earlier chapters, the education debate from 1976 onwards has been dominated by concern for alleged declining standards. Universities also made it known that it would be difficult to accept N and F and also produce honours graduates in only three years. In 1979 the Schools Council published a progress report but, in March 1979 the Secretary of State, Shirley Williams, announced that A levels would not be abolished, because there was not enough agreement on alternative proposals. Thus one of the effects of the 'Great Debate' was to delay progress on the 16–18 curriculum for several years.

With the change of government in 1979, the new Conservative Secretary of State, Mark Carlisle, indicated support for the retention of A levels as guarantees of high standards. The Schools Council were, however, asked to continue their studies of a curriculum for non-A level 16–19-year-olds. In December 1979, the Schools Council suggested yet another solution to the A level problem: an Intermediate ('I' level) examination for students with O level Grade C or better; the I level course was designed to be the equivalent of about half an A level, taken over a two-year period. The Schools Council suggested that I levels plus the Certificate of Extended Education (CEE – see below) would provide suitable courses for all non-A level sixth formers. The government published a Consultative Document in October 1980 which encouraged the notion of I level examinations provided they were only on offer to candidates also taking at least two A levels at the same time (DES, 1980c), but this was effectively a rejection of the original idea.

Criticisms of A levels continued in the early 1980s. In May 1984, the government, whilst continuing to maintain support for A levels, called for an adjustment to the structure by the introduction of Advanced Supplementary (AS) level examinations. AS levels are intended to require half the study time of A levels; they will enable students to widen their subject choices by replacing one or more A levels by a larger number of AS levels. AS levels will be either 'complementary' – i.e. fitting in with their main 'A level subjects, or 'contrasting' subjects. AS level courses were introduced from September 1987 and will be examined in 1989.

In March 1987, the Secretary of State appointed a Committee, chaired by Dr Gordon Higginson, Vice-Chancellor of the University of Southampton, to 'recommend the principles that should govern A level syllabuses and their assessment'.

The Higginson Report: Advancing A Levels

Many felt that Dr Higginson had been given a very difficult task: radical changes to 16–19 curriculum and examinations were clearly necessary, but his brief was limited to an examination of A levels which seemed to regard the form of that examination as sacrosanct. The Higginson Report, *Advancing A Levels* (DES, 1988e) began with an interesting comparison of A levels with what happened in other industrial countries:

> The French Baccalaureat, for example, lasts for three years and is a multi-subject examination. Typically, candidates take written and oral examinations in seven subjects. In the USA the High School Diploma requires that, of

the subjects studied, seven (English, social studies, mathematics, science, a foreign language and health and physical education) are compulsory. The German Abitur consists of four subjects with written examinations in two main subjects and an optional subject, and an oral examination in a second option. Candidates must include study of a modern foreign language, mathematics or natural science, and German. The grading system takes account of course work as well as the final examination. (Para. 1.2)

The Report went on to recommend a five subject A level, with 'leaner and tougher' syllabuses and more emphasis on understanding – less emphasis on 'cramming facts'. The Report was generally welcomed by educationists but was rejected by the Secretary of State, Mr Baker, allegedly under direct pressure from the Prime Minister. The reasons given for the rejection (or limited acceptance) of the Report were explained in an answer to a parliamentary question on the publication of the Higginson Report:

> We broadly welcome the general principles for A levels set out by the Committee in Chapter 2 of its Report and, in particular, its endorsement of A levels as demanding, single subject examinations for able candidates of all kinds and all backgrounds. We have reservations, however, on the Committee's detailed proposals for steamlining syllabuses by reducing their factual content.
>
> The Report indicates widespread support for increased breadth of study for 16–18-year-olds undertaking A level courses in full-time education. It recommends that such students should, if possible, study five subjects, some at A level and some at AS level and, to allow for study of more subjects, that A level syllabuses should be streamlined, and that students should devote more of their timetables to examination studies.
>
> The government endorses the general aim of broadening A level students' programmes of study but does not accept the Committee's proposals for achieving that objective through a five subject programme incorporating leaner A level syllabuses. The education service already has a substantial agenda for reform: we want the new Secondary Examinations and Assessment Council in particular to concentrate on the tasks of introducing assessment and testing arrangements for the national curriculum and of the establishment, monitoring and review of GCSE. We see AS levels as the key to achieving greater breadth and hence we welcome the Committee's backing for a continuing role for these new examinations, both in securing breadth of study and in supplementing main areas of study. Following the introduction of AS levels last year, A level students, by choosing a mix of A and AS level syllabuses, are already able to put together broader and more balanced programmes of study. The government will continue to monitor closely the introduction and take-up of AS levels and will consider, in the light of progress, whether further steps are needed to secure the necessary broadening of post-16 education. (DES Press Release, 7 June 1988)

The acceptance of the Higginson Report might not have solved the problem: it would, for example, have been possible for a science student to have taken five science subjects, thus avoiding the aim of balance. It now seems that progress towards a better curriculum must take the form of developing AS level courses.

Non-A level courses 16–19

So far, I have been discussing the massive and hitherto unsolved problem of finding a suitable curriculum and examination for those academic boys and girls who intend to proceed to higher education; but there is an equally important problem of devising a suitable education programme for those who are less academic or who do not intend moving directly from school to university or college. What kind of programme should be provided for them?

Certificate of Extended Education (CEE)

Brief reference has already been made to the CEE. This was a worthy attempt to find a qualification suitable for 17-year-olds who had achieved Grades 2–4 at CSE and pursued one year's study in the sixth form. This seemed to be a promising development of CSE style syllabuses and forms of assessment; it was taught on an experimental basis from 1976, and examined by groups of CSE and GCE Boards. The Keohane Report (1979c) recommended that there should be a modification to the single subject nature of the examination and that there should be a compulsory examination of a core syllabus of numerical and communications skills. However, the Report was not accepted by the Conservative Government. Instead, the DES document *Examinations 16–18* (DES, 1980c) suggested a closer relationship between employment and courses of study for 17+ students. A later discussion paper from the DES *17+ A new qualification* (DES, 1982) took up suggestions from the Further Education Unit (FEU) and moulded them into courses for the Certificate of Pre-Vocational Education (CPVE) which began in September 1983. The CEE will cease to operate after 1988.

Certificate of Pre-Vocational Education (CPVE)

CPVE was developed not by examining boards but by the DES. The Certificate began in 1985, after some pilot schemes in 1984 had been evaluated by FEU. The intention of CPVE is to encourage students in FE and schools to prepare for the world of work, and to establish a basis of study from which successful students can progress to other national qualifications. The CPVE includes an element of general education related to practical and vocational concerns. The structure consists of three components:

1 An integrated core of basic skills needed for adult and working life.
2 Vocational studies.
3 Additional studies (e.g. community activities, recreational courses etc.) which take 25 per cent of the students' time.

Examination Reform for Schools (DES, 1987b)

CPVE is not administered by the GCE and GCSE Boards but by the City and Guilds of London Institute (CGLI) and the Business and Technician Education Council (BTEC) through the Joint Board for Pre-Vocational Education. A major reason for the introduction of CPVE in 1985 was to replace the large number of pre-vocational courses on offer by a single system; but it is still possible, for example, for 16-year-olds to enrol direct for BTEC courses. A further attempt to rationalise post-16 vocational courses was the establishment of the National Council for Vocational Qualifications (NCVQ) in July 1986. This Council is not an examining board, but functions as an organisation for establishing national criteria and then accrediting those qualifications provided by other bodies which meet those criteria. NCVQ was set up by the Department of Employment, but the DES is responsible for giving the Council educational advice and direction. The powers of the Secretary of State for Education were strengthened by the 1988 Education Act.

OTHER SCHOOL EXAMINATIONS/METHODS OF ASSESSMENT

The 1988 Act permits pupils up to the age of 16 to study in school only for qualifications specifically approved by the Secretary of State. The main intention of this was to establish GCSE and national assessment at 16+ as the means of evaluating the national curriculum. It remains to be seen whether some other qualifications might be regarded as acceptable. However, even within the national curriculum/GCSE framework, there have been interesting developments in recent years.

Graded tests/graded assessments

The first graded assessment schemes began in the 1970s: groups of modern language teachers, dissatisfied with conventional methods of examining in GCE and CSE, attempted to devise assessment schemes more appropriate for their subject. Graded assessment schemes were usually planned as five-year courses but with candidates progressing through the grades at their own pace. Some of the early schemes were treated as 'Mode 3' examinations by the examining boards, and considerable success was claimed in terms of pupil motivation (graded assessment schemes in foreign languages were evaluated by HMI in 1983). A major influence behind the idea of graded assessment was the well-established tradition of graded tests in musical performance run by the Royal Schools of Music.

Some examining boards have also developed graded assessment in other subject areas such as mathematics, science, craft design technology, and – more controversially – English. Mary Warnock (1988) was so captivated by the idea of graded tests that she has advocated replacing the whole of the secondary curriculum by graded tests. However, this is to make the crucial mistake, very common in discussions of curriculum and assessment, of assuming that because a scheme works well for one part of the curriculum that it can be applied to everything else. Graded assessment functions successfully in those areas of learning where *skills* are very important. Thus modern languages benefit from this approach, but it would be more difficult, perhaps impossible, to apply graded tests to poetry appreciation or historical understanding. Nevertheless, it seems safe to assume that graded assessment will remain as a useful part of the assessment pattern of the national curriculum – but limited to certain areas.

Records of achievement/pupil profiles

Records of achievement or profiles represent another indication of the increasing public concern for the evaluation of pupils' performance and progress. I noted earlier in this chapter that the idea of a record of achievement goes back at least as far as the Norwood Report (1943). Twenty years later the need was reaffirmed in the Newsom Report: 'Boys and girls who stay at school until they are 16 may reasonably look for some record of achievement when they leave'. (*Half Our Future*, 1963, Chapter 10). However, another twenty years passed before the DES drew attention to the fact that 'Most young people leave school after eleven or more years of education with no comprehensive records of their educational attainments'. (DES, July 1984). In the same 'Statement of Policy' it was pointed out that many LEAs and schools used records of achievement or profiles, and that records played an important part in TVEI schemes and other more vocationally organised programmes. But there was a confusing variety of practices and forms of presentation; a more uniform national approach was clearly needed – but not, it was stressed, a straitjacket.

The DES Statement of Policy (1984) outlined four main purposes for records of achievement:

1 Acknowledgment and recognition of effort and achievement.
2 Motivation and personal development (including increasing the pupils' awareness of their own strengths, weaknesses and opportunities).
3 Schools would identify more clearly the aims and objectives of their own curriculum and organisation.
4 A document of record which school leavers would have for employers and others.

Pilot schemes were established which would be evaluated and reported on in the Autumn of 1988, so that all schools would have sufficient guidance on the requirements for records of achievement which would have to be provided for all school leavers in the early 1990s.

Although these arrangements for records of achievement were set up before the establishment of the national curriculum, they should be seen as part of the same trend: greater accountability to the centre and better feedback for pupils. Schools will be required to operate a national curriculum which includes a national scheme of assessment; but other important learning and development takes place in schools which should be on record for pupils, parents, employers and others. The Norwood Report's good idea of a School Leaving Ceritficate supplemented by much more comprehensive records will eventually be put into operation – after only fifty years of discussion!

SUMMARY

For a long time secondary schools in England have used examinations as a substitute for having a well-planned curriculum with built-in assessment procedures in each school. This tradition has led to at least three weaknesses: first, the lack of clear overall aims and objectives for the school, including curriculum objectives; second, the absence of adequate assessment procedures for those pupils not taking traditional external examinations; third, the domination of the school organisation by the 'needs' of a small minority of pupils proceeding to higher education.

It is taking a long time for secondary schools in England and Wales to break away from that tradition. Successive reports such as Norwood, (1943), Crowther (1959), Newsom (1963) and others including HMI surveys have complained, but only recently has effective action been taken to establish clear curriculum and assessment guidelines to enable schools to perceive external examinations in a less dominating way. The Schools Council missed an opportunity to deal with the question of the whole curriculum, and unfortunately they were thwarted in their attempts to reform examinations at 16+ and 18+. An enlightened approach to the national curriculum, and national assessment including GCSE, may now go some way towards dealing with the problem 11–16, but 16–18 remains problematic unless the development of AS levels can be stimulated.

Since 1976, partly because of the lack of clear curriculum policies, another danger has appeared: the tendency to exaggerate the vocational function of secondary schooling, and this has been reflected in the structure of examinations. This tendency may be resisted by sensible implementation of the national curriculum and GCSE, but there will be a need for constant vigilance to prevent that kind of curriculum distortion.

FUTURE DEVELOPMENTS:
9 | CURRICULUM CHANGE AND THE ROLE OF THE TEACHER

Since the 1981 HMI reports on schools have been published; even before that, we had the benefit of the independent critical voice of HMI in the form of their Primary and Secondary Surveys (DES, 1978a and 1979a). They had drawn attention to the fact that many schools lack appropriate planning procedures for the curriculum, and do not have satisfactory statements of curricular aims and objectives. My own analysis, in earlier chapters of this book, goes somewhat futher. In my view, curriculum planning is generally flawed by being based on an incomplete selection from the culture of our society: specifically, schools frequently omit, for large numbers of pupils, political, economic, moral and aesthetic understanding and awareness.

This inadequate selection from the culture exists partly for historical reasons – schools tend to change less quickly than other aspects of society, hence the problem referred to by some educationists as 'cultural lag and curriculum inertia'. One aspect of this inertia is the reliance on a limited range of traditional subjects as the delivery system for a curriculum which ought now to be much more complex.

The proposals for a national curriculum, including national assessment, will probably go some way towards improving the curriculum in many schools, but it will be difficult to solve the problem completely by this means, because the national curriculum is to be subject based. Much will depend on the ingenuity of the subject group planners responsible for 'programmes of study' within the national curriculum: they may be able to repair some of the damage, by filling in gaps between subjects with cross-curricular work – perhaps in the form of modules in health education, economic understanding and so on. However, it is likely that much will be left for individual schools to plan, within the general structure of the national curriculum. It will be very important for schools to make the most of the opportunity presented by the implementation of a national curriculum during the 1990s. They should consider not simply changes in curriculum content, but should also re-examine the whole teaching-learning process in the school as part of curriculum analysis.

THE CHANGING ROLE OF THE TEACHER

What is very clear from discussions of the national curriculum is that more will be asked of teachers, and that teachers will need to make adjustments to their traditional role. The implementation of curricular reforms and changes in assessment makes it necessary for teachers to have a wider range of skills and improved opportunities for professional development. Teaching traditional curricula was in many respects much easier: the teacher possessed certain knowledge (mostly factual information) which had to be learned and reproduced by pupils. The teacher's task was to present the information in manageable packages, the pupils memorised the information, and after an interval the teacher tested the pupils' recall. Correct and incorrect answers could easily be identified and pupils given a mark without difficulty.

Reformed curricula and assessment procedures, however, may be pedagogically more difficult in several ways. There is less emphasis on memorisation of content and more concern with understanding 'process': for example, in history less stress on dates and narrative but more on understanding lifestyles of people living in earlier epochs and the causes of historic events. For such learning to be effective, the teacher has to have greater understanding of the subject matter. This is partly a question of insight into the 'structure' of the discipline or subject, including the ability to identify key concepts, ideas and generalisations. Teachers must also be able to transmit this more abstract knowledge to the pupils, which is much more difficult than the presentation of facts to be stored. Some new curricula also involve more active styles of pupil learning, for example, acquiring and practising historical skills rather than the simple passive learning of second-hand materials. Giving pupils the opportunity to 'solve historical problems' by working with documents, presents pedagogical problems and also potentially greater difficulties of classroom organisation and control – it is easier for pupil behaviour to get out of hand and for the teacher to lose control over the learning situation.

Not only are new curricula and teaching methods more difficult to handle, but teachers also have to face the prospect of criticism from parents and other members of the public for failing to teach 'real' subject matter. For example, the new General Certificate of Secondary Education (GCSE), examined for the first time in 1988, included 'empathy' as a small part of the new history syllabus. In the early months of 1988 there was a public campaign denouncing teachers for departing from traditional views of what counted as history.

Another aspect of the problem is that reforms may be in advance of initial teacher training, so that teachers are rarely completely prepared for the new curriculum in their pre-service professional courses. Also, there are other problems of an even more complex kind: for example, it has been suggested that some new science curricula went too far in the direction of 'discovery learning' with not enough attention being paid to the need to acquire some knowledge 'second-hand', that is, by being told. Some have also argued that the condemnation of 'mere memorisation' has similarly been overstated (Mathews, 1985). There are important distinctions to be made between memorisation without understanding, acquiring knowledge by traditional didactic methods but with a grasp of its significance, and learning experientially. Because experiential learning is excellent for some aspects of the curriculum, however, it does not follow that all learning must be active and experiential. Even if it were feasible to organise a curriculum in that way, it would not always be desirable to do so. Teachers have sometimes been encouraged to operate new curricula without thoroughly examining the principles on which the innovations were based.

Thus it is all too easy for teachers to become disillusioned with the new curricula – perhaps because they had not been adequately prepared; perhaps because the curriculum itself was not sufficiently well-planned and tested before implementation. Two solutions have been proposed: first, more and better in-service courses; second, more curriculum development which is at least partly school-based. This is not to suggest that the centre-periphery or 'top down' models of curriculum development are completely out-moded: it is a question of balance. It would be unreasonable to expect every school to develop its own curriculum from first principles, but it would be equally foolish to attempt to impose a detailed, uniform curriculum on every school, leaving no room for school-based development geared to specific local needs.

THE STATUS OF THE TEACHER

Ironically, in recent years, at a time when the task of teaching has become more complex and difficult, there has been a tendency for teachers to be criticised more and respected less. For example, teachers have been blamed for a range of social problems from school leavers being ill-prepared for the world of work to juvenile delinquency and drug-taking. At the same time, teachers have tended not to keep pace with other middle-class groups in terms of salaries and improved conditions of service.

The problem is not confined to England: in a review of the literature on teacher evaluation, Darling-Hammond *et al.* (1983) examined the role of the teacher from the point of view of 'conceptions of teacher work', and suggested four views of the work of teachers existing in the minds of politicians and administrators: teaching as routine labour, craft, profession, or art. These four conceptions of 'teacher work' are ideal types, not to be found in a pure form in the real world; but the way that politicians, administrators and others regard teaching, and the way that they want teachers to be appraised, may be closely related to one or other of those four categories. Moreover, in any discussion of the role of the teacher, it is essential to clarify and make explicit prevailing assumptions about 'teacher work'. Underlying many open disputes about teachers' salaries and conditions of service, there are covert disagreements between employers who regard teaching as 'labour' or 'craft', and teachers who want to be treated as 'professionals' or 'artists'.

New kinds of responsibilities associated with changes in curriculum and assessment can either be seen as adding to the burden of 'routine workers' or as giving teachers even greater possibilities for extending their professional role. To some extent how teachers are regarded depends on how they react to new developments, but the attitudes of employing authorities are clearly very important. If teachers are expected to take on new responsibilities and acquire new skills it is essential that they are not treated in other respects more like routine workers. It is particularly demoralising for teachers to receive conflicting signals – that is, to be expected to take on professional responsibilities at the same time as being downgraded in other respects.

In this context, it is important that teacher appraisal should be seen as part of the process of professional development rather than as an opportunity for reducing numbers of teaching staff. If teachers are subject to campaigns of public criticism they will tend to resist any proposal to assess teaching ability – seeing it as a threat rather than as a means of staff development. Ways have to be found of showing teachers that they enjoy public confidence in what they are doing as well as high prestige for performing a task which demands difficult professional abilities.

Most countries introducing curriculum reform and new methods of assessment run the risk of overloading teachers. For example, the new GCSE is in danger of over-burdening teachers with paperwork. One study has estimated that, on average, the teachers' workload is increased by about five hours each week. This may be an extreme case, but all new forms of assessment tend to increase the teachers' workload, and there is evidence that teachers, despite the popular image of their enjoying short working days and long holidays, are already overburdened.

A NEW KIND OF TEACHER?

The new national curriculum is likely to transform the role of the teacher, gradually but very significantly. The good teacher will no longer be just an efficient instructor, but will have to become an expert classroom manager and organiser of learning experiences. The specific kinds of changes that will arise include the teacher as an expert in curriculum design, and as an expert in assessment and record-keeping.

I have elsewhere (1983) suggested that curriculum planning (and curriculum control) should be seen as a question of power-sharing and division of responsibilities according to the level of specificity involved. I suggested that it would be appropriate to envisage five levels of responsibility:

1	National (DES – NCC)	general guidelines.
2	Regional (LEAs)	implementation and coordination.
3	Institutional (the school)	whole curriculum
4	Departmental (teaching teams)	syllabuses and programmes.
5	Individual (teacher)	lesson planning.

This means that individual teachers will not simply put into operation a curriculum designed elsewhere; the teacher has limited 'ownership' of the curriculum and is directly responsible for the detailed planning of lessons within national and LEA guidelines, bearing in mind the specific needs of his or her pupils, as well as the local aspects of the curriculum as planned by the school. To do this effectively, teachers will need to be more than transmitters of their own subject.

THE QUALITIES OF A PROFESSIONAL TEACHER

A good professional teacher will be able to relate his or her own teaching responsibilities to the whole curriculum. This has two dimensions: first, subject sequence or diachronic integration; second, inter-subject or synchronic integration. That is, the teacher should relate the current year's teaching assignment with what was covered the previous year, and with what will follow next year. That may sound obvious, but it is often ignored. Accusations about needless repetition of subject-matter are not entirely without foundation. The good teacher will also relate her own teaching assignment (e.g. mathematics) to the responsibilities of other teachers (e.g. the mathematics involved in physics or geography etc.). The professional teacher will not only know what other teachers are doing, but will plan a teaching programme to complement theirs. Primary teachers will be particularly concerned with diachronic integration, whereas secondary teachers should be concerned with both, but are often likely to neglect synchronic integration.

Apart from diachronic integration, teachers will also be concerned with achieving the best sequence of learning within any one year or term. Bruner's concept of the shuffle test may be useful (i.e. if you change the order of presentation of the sections of a syllabus and it makes no difference, then perhaps it should!). Teachers must also be able to diagnose the problems and difficulties of individual pupils, keep records of them, attempt alternative strategies of teaching, and record successes and failures. Apart from differences in intelligence, which may be related to learning speed, there are other personality differences in learning style which are sometimes ignored by teachers, or only treated at an intuitive level. The professional teacher will be able to categorise individual pupils in a variety of ways and teach accordingly. Thus, teachers need to have a repertoire of teaching styles as well as the ability to diagnose individual differences in learning – including problems of understanding.

Professional teachers will also be much more expert in assessment techniques and in recording those results in a meaningful way. The TGAT proposals for assessing the national curriculum (see Chapter 7) place considerable responsibilities on teachers. Teachers will have the initial task of deciding – as part of the process of continuous assessment – which level is the appropriate one for each pupil. Then the teacher will carry out the designated national assessment procedures, and become involved in complex moderating exercises. All of this assumes that teachers will be familiar with assessment methods and the related statistical principles.

Record keeping

In addition to the continuous assessment records necessary for the national curriculum procedures, from the early 1990s *all* teachers will be required to operate with 'records of achievement' for all pupils. If this is not to become a meaningless bureaucratic exercise, teachers will need to develop more sophisticated record-keeping skills, including discussions with pupils, and be prepared to justify their judgements with parents and others.

If the DES attempts to operate the national curriculum, national assessment and records of achievement with untrained, amateur teachers, this could well be a recipe for disaster. Perhaps the most important lesson of the 1960s was that no curriculum development was possible without teacher development. All the indications point towards the need to develop a much more professional teaching force.

The language of curriculum and pedagogy

One of the requirements for professional teachers is that they should be familiar with some specialists technical vocabulary and its usage. For example: the difference between aims, goals and objectives (behavioural and non-behavioural); the meaning of assessment and appraisal; the many meanings of standards; competence and competency-based teaching; the core curriculum, common curriculum, uniform curriculum (all of which require an understanding of the concept of culture). They will need to be sensitive to the difference between process and product; the difference between criterion-referenced and norm-referenced testing; the difference between diagnostic evaluation and standardised testing; formative and summative evaluation; and the distinctions between knowledge, skills and values. Teachers should also be able to define literacy, numeracy, oracy and computer literacy; to distinguish between syllabus, programme of work, curriculum; and to understand reliability and validity in the context of tests and test items.

This is, of course, by no means a comprehensive list. It is merely a small selection from the concepts which should be available to professional teachers.

School-based curriculum development and evaluation

Teachers are, however, not just individuals; much of the curriculum development described in this book assumes the existence of teams of teachers working cooperatively in schools. One of the results of the search for ways to improve quality in schools has been a tendency to focus on school-based curriculum development and various kinds of school-based evaluation. This interest has developed for a number of sometimes conflicting reasons: the first was a reaction against the centre-periphery model of planning, evaluation and implementation which came under more and more critical scrutiny in the 1970s. The second reason is that the increasing desire of teachers to be treated as professionals rather than as state functionaries, has encouraged a tendency to look for ways in which teachers could solve their own professional problems at a local level rather than react to more remote initiatives. Hence the emphasis on the school as the obvious location for curriculum renewal, the in-service education of teachers, the evaluation of teaching and learning, and even educational research. A third factor is the tendency to demand greater accountability in education including the need to render accounts to the central authority.

One assumption of this chapter is that the trend to school-based activities of many kinds is generally beneficial to teachers, pupils and the educational service as a whole; but it is also necessary to sound a note of caution: the school-based movement occasionally leads to excesses. Extreme statements are sometimes made about decentralisation where the impression is given that the only kinds of innovation which are desirable or even permissible are those which are entirely school-based. This chapter argues for a more balanced attitude.

A second danger is that school-based activities – especially evaluation – can lead to developments completely contrary to the declared aims and intentions of school-based innovation. Such evaluation can easily become, for example, part of very mechanistic accountability exercises on a regional or national scale which have the effect of tying teachers down to rigid requirements or guidelines rather than being able to develop the potential for creative innovation.

School-based evaluation is neither a simple process nor an uncontroversial one. Throughout this book reference has been made to two major opposing pressures – teacher professionalism and accountability. These tend to push school-based evaluation in two different directions; but Nuttall (1986) has suggested that compromise is possible, whilst Rodger and Richardson (1985) see school-based evaluation as a means of resolving those tensions:

> It is argued here that the process by which schools become self-evaluating is a means by which a suitable compromise between the demands for accountability and the increasing professionalisation of school staff can be reached. The self-evaluating school can be seen as an institution in which the genuinely professional activities of reflection and self-appraisal are carried on whilst, at the same time, the kind of information demanded by advocates of educational accountability will be systematically collected and used within the school in order to inform policy-making. How the school will use information gathered via self-evaluation programmes will be a matter of debate and will reflect the requirements of the local situation. But it remains the case that the school which

can be seen to be professionally accountable in the sense that it engages in procedures which involve asking fundamental questions about policy, organisation and curricula is less likely to suffer the extreme forms of being called to account implied by a rigorous application of the accountability model for schools. There is evidence of a general recognition that schools need to become self-evaluating if they are to retain both public esteem and the capacity to change in an increasingly difficult financial and political climate. (p. 9)

Other writers, especially those familiar with US experience and research (for example, Darling-Hammond *et al.*, 1983) are less optimistic.

At the same time as schools are being required to embark upon the national curriculum, they are also being encouraged to take on greater direct responsibilities for financial and other aspects of school management. The 1988 Act includes provision for the 'local management of schools' (LMS). The thrust of this development, which some see as a disguised cost-cutting exercise, is to give schools more financial autonomy; but as the discussion of the scheme has progressed nationally, the description has changed from 'local financial management' (LFM) to 'local management of schools' (LMS). This is intended to convey the political intention to decentralise the management of schools (away from LEAs) and give them more autonomy, including limited financial control.

Some kinds of local management, when tried on an experimental basis in some LEAs, have proved to be beneficial to the schools. However, there are dangers: it is important for more cooperative work, including curriculum development, to take place *within* schools, but it is also important not to neglect cooperation *between* schools, including the dicussion of new curriculum ideas and their implementation. Some of the best local curriculum development in the past took place with groups of schools organised by LEAs. It will also be desirable for schools to avoid allowing LMS to make them so inward-looking that they lose contact with university departments of education and other higher education institutions. There is a need for education theory to be generated from practice, but that does not mean that the traditional educational disciplines do not have much to offer in illuminating the theory generated from practice.

THE PRACTICAL TASK OF IMPLEMENTING THE NATIONAL CURRICULUM AT SCHOOL LEVEL

It may be useful to conclude this book by analysing, stage by stage, what a school staff would need to do in order to implement the national curriculum.

Stage 1 – Aims

There is a danger that schools will be tempted simply to accept the national curriculum in the form of a list of subjects, assessment tasks and programmes of study, and try to put them directly into operation. This would be to ignore the point I referred to in Chapter 4, also made by Malcolm Skilbeck, that it is necessary to go back at least one stage before converting objectives into teaching programmes.

The first task for a school staff to undertake will be to discuss the aims of the school. This is essential, but dangerous – it could take years to reach complete agreement. It will be better to impose a time limit on this discussion, work towards as much consensus as possible, and list disagreements for resolution (if possible) at later stages.

Teachers will certainly want to look at the DES list of aims derived from the *Framework for the School Curriculum* (DES, 1980a) but revised in *Better Schools* (DES, 1985a):

1 To help pupils to develop lively, enquiring minds, the ability to question and argue rationally and to apply themselves to tasks, and physical skills.
2 To help pupils to acquire understanding, knowledge and skills relevant to adult life and employment in a fast-changing world.
3 To help pupils to use language and number effectively.
4 To help pupils to develop personal moral values, respect for religious values, and tolerance of other races, religions, and ways of life.
5 To help pupils to understand the world in which they live, and the inter-dependence of individuals, groups and nations.
6 To help pupils to appreciate human achievements and aspirations.

Teachers are likely to come to the conclusion that these aims are generally acceptable but not sufficiently specific for detailed curriculum planning.

Stage 2 – Cultural analysis: core and foundation subjects

The next stage will be to look at the proposed list of subjects for the national curriculum (core and foundation) and discuss their adequacy for a delivery system for the aims referred to above. This could involve the kind of cultural analysis which I have employed in Chapter 3 (but not necessarily using my model – teachers might prefer to use the HMI 'Areas of Learning and Experience' (DES, 1977c and 1985b). The discussion should lead naturally to the adequacy of the ten subjects as a method of *delivering* the desired curriculum. This stage will include looking at 'programmes of study' provided by subject working groups to see what is included and how they can best be converted into teaching and learning schemes.

National Curriculum Subjects:

English
Mathematics

Science
Technology
Foreign language
History
Geography
Art/Music/Drama/Design
Physical Education
(Religious Education is taken for granted)

Stage 3 – Identifying gaps

The discussion of the core and foundation subjects listed above will highlight the fact that not all desirable content will emerge automatically from a simple list of subjects. The Consultation Document itself refers to cross-curricular work needed to cover such areas as health education. If the staff agree to some extent with my analysis they will add political, economic and moral education to the list of desirable areas to be covered. If so, they should be as specific as possible, using secondary sources wherever necessary (much work has been done in each of those fields, so it will not be necessary for every school to work out the detailed programmes from first principles).

Stage 4 – Filling gaps

The teachers then have to decide, given the particular nature of the school, its local environment and catchment area, how best to fill the gaps identified in Stage 3 above. This will be a question of tactics rather than grand strategy but none the less important for that. Some schools which have already gone through this process (before the national curriculum) found that it was helpful to think in terms of a more flexible timetable (there is a good deal of discussion of problems and opportunities in Moon, 1988).

Stage 5 – The timetable

Having agreed on possible solutions, it will be necessary to put them into operation by means of a revised timetable. Once again, making use of the experiences of other schools will avoid learning the hard way. The task has been made simpler by the availability of computer software.

Stage 6 – Evaluation

It will be essential to give teachers an opportunity to discuss progress, and if necessary to make changes. As part of the evaluation process it is sometimes an advantage to bring in a suitably qualified, sympathetic outsider: not only does this reassure parents and governors, but an experienced non-participant can often see problems and offer solutions which would be difficult for anyone inside the institution (see Roger and Richardson, 1985).

SUMMARY

Many teachers who were particularly interested in curriculum were disappointed that the 1987–88 proposals for a national curriculum were based on an old-fashioned, 'school-subject' model. Throughout the debate on the Education Reform Bill many remained critical. However, the national curriculum was largely unchanged in the 1988 Act and has now become a legal requirement. The National Curriculum Council (NCC) created by the Act will have responsibility for keeping the national curriculum up to date, but meanwhile schools have to get on with the task of implementing the subject-based curriculum in the best way possible.

It has been suggested in this chapter that most teachers are conscientious professionals who will face up to this challenge as successfully as secondary school teachers coped with GCSE from 1986 to 1988, despite the difficulties involved and the inadequate provision for training. This book has attempted to suggest some approaches to curriculum planning and implementation which may be helpful. However, those responsible for implementation, nationally and locally, should not underestimate the magnitude of the task of putting into operation a completely new national curriculum together with a national assessment programme. Adequate resources, planning time and opportunities for professional development and training will be essential.

Appendix – Fifty Years of Curriculum Change

1938   Spens Report (Grammer and Technical Schools)
1943   Norwood Report (Curriculum and Examinations)
1944   Butler Education Act
1951   GCE Replaces School Certificate
1959   Crowther Report (15–18)
1962   Curriculum Study Group
1963   Newsom Report
1964   Lockwood Report: Schools Council
1964   Ministry of Education transformed into Department of Education and Science (DES)
1965   DES Circular 10/65 (Comprehensive Schools)
1967   Plowden Report (Primary Schools)
1972   White Paper *Education: A Framework for Expansion*
1974   Assessment of Performance Unit (APU)
1975   Bullock Report (*A Language for Life*)
1976   Callaghan's Ruskin speech
1976   The Great Debate
1977   Green Paper *Education in Schools: A Consultative Document*
1977   *Curriculum 11–16* (HMI)
1978   HMI Primary Survey
1978   Waddell Report (Recommending common examination at 16+)
1978   Warnock Report (Children with special needs)
1979   HMI Secondary Survey
1980   Education Act (Parents' Charter)
1980   *A Framework for the School Curriculum* (DES)
1980   *A View of the Curriculum* (HMI)
1981   Education Act (Special Educational Needs)
1981   *The School Curriculum* (DES)
1983   Schools Council abolished and replaced by Secondary Examinations Council (SEC) and School Curriculum Development Committee (SCDC)
1984   Sir Keith Joseph's North of England speech
1985   *Curriculum 5–16* (HMI series *Curriculum Matters*)
1985   *Better Schools* (DES)
1986   Education Act
1987   Kenneth Baker's North of England speech
1987   Education Reform Bill
1988   Education Reform Act

Bibliography

ACKERMAN, B.A. (1980) *Social Justice in the Liberal State.* New Haven, Conn: Yale University Press.

ANDERSON, D. (1988) *Full Circle?* London: Social Affairs Unit.

ARNOLD, M. (1869) *Culture and Anarchy.* Cambridge: Cambridge University Press.

AULD, R. (1976) 'William Tyndale Junior and Infants School Report of Public Enquiry conducted... into the Teaching and Organisation and Management of the William Tyndale Junior and Infants Schools', Islington, London N1. London: Inner London Education Authority.

BARNETT, C. (1986) *The Audit of War.* London: MacMillan.

BENEDICT, R. (1934) *Patterns of Culture.* (various editions)

BOARD OF EDUCATION (1905, 1929, 1937) *Handbook of Suggestions for the Consideration of Teachers and Others Concerned with the Work of Public Elementary Schools.* London: HMSO.

BOARD OF EDUCATION (1938) *Report of the Consultative Committee on Secondary Education with special reference to Grammar Schools and Technical High Schools* (Spens Report) London: HMSO.

BOARD OF EDUCATION (1943) *Curriculum and Examinations in Secondary Schools: Report of the Committee of the Secondary School Examinations Council* (Norwood Report). London: HMSO.

BOBBITT, F. (1918) *The Curriculum.* Boston, Mass: Houghton Mifflin.

BOBBITT, F. (1924) *How to Make a Curriculum.* Boston, Mass: Houghton Mifflin.

BUTTON, L. (1981, 1982) *Group Tutoring for the Form Teacher: 1 Lower Secondary School, 2 Upper Secondary School.* London: Hodder and Stoughton.

CENTRAL ADVISORY COUNCIL FOR EDUCATION (CACE) (1963) Report of CACE: *Half our Future* (Newsom Report). London: HMSO.

CENTRAL ADVISORY COUNCIL FOR EDUCATION (CACE) 1967 *Children and their Primary Schools* (The Plowden Report). London: HMSO.

CORBETT, A. (1976) *Whose Schools?* London: Faber Research Services.

COX, C.B. and DYSON, A.E. (eds) (1969) *Fight for Education: A Black Paper.* London: Critical Quarterly Society.

DARLING-HAMMOND, L., WISE, A.E. and PEASE, S.R. (1983) 'Teacher Evaluation in the Organisational Context' *Review of Educational Research,* **53**, 3, 285–328.

DEARDEN, R.F. (1968) *Philosophy of Primary School Education.* London: Routledge and Kegan Paul.

DEPARTMENT OF EDUCATION AND SCIENCE (1964) *Working Party on Schools Curricula and Examinations* (Lockwood Report), London: HMSO.

DEPARTMENT OF EDUCATION AND SCIENCE (1965) Circular 10/65 *The Organisation of Secondary Education.* London: HMSO.

DEPARTMENT OF EDUCATION AND SCIENCE (1972) White Paper *Education: A Framework for Expansion*. London: HMSO.

DEPARTMENT OF EDUCATION AND SCIENCE (1975) *A Language for Life* (Bullock Report) London: HMSO.

DEPARTMENT OF EDUCATION AND SCIENCE (1976) *Ten Good Schools: A Secondary School Enquiry* (HMI Matters for Discussion Document 1). London: HMSO.

DEPARTMENT OF EDUCATION AND SCIENCE (1977a) *Education in Schools: A Consultative Document* (Green Paper), London: HMSO.

DEPARTMENT OF EDUCATION AND SCIENCE (1977b) Circular 14/77 *Local Authority Arrangements for the School Curriculum*. London: HMSO.

DEPARTMENT OF EDUCATION AND SCIENCE (1977c) *Curriculum 11–16*, Working Papers by HMI. London: HMSO

DEPARTMENT OF EDUCATION AND SCIENCE (1978a) *Primary Education in England*. A Survey by HMI. London: HMSO

DEPARTMENT OF EDUCATION AND SCIENCE (1978b) *Special Educational Needs* (Warnock Report). London: HMSO.

DEPARTMENT OF EDUCATION AND SCIENCE (1978c) *Steering Committee on a Common System of Examining at 16+* (School Examinations Parts I and II (Waddell Report). London: HMSO.

DEPARTMENT OF EDUCATION AND SCIENCE (1978d) *Secondary School Examinations: A Single System at 16+*. London: HMSO.

DEPARTMENT OF EDUCATION AND SCIENCE (1979a) *Aspects of Secondary Education*: A Survey by H M Inspectors of Schools. London: HMSO.

DEPARTMENT OF EDUCATION AND SCIENCE (1979b) *Local Authority Arrangements for the School Curriculum*. London: HMSO.

DEPARTMENT OF EDUCATION AND SCIENCE (1979c) *Proposals for a Certificate of Extended Education* (Keohane Report). London: HMSO.

DEPARTMENT OF EDUCATION AND SCIENCE (1980a) *A Framework for the School Curriculum*. London: HMSO.

DEPARTMENT OF EDUCATION AND SCIENCE (1980b) *A View of the Curriculum*. London: HMSO.

DEPARTMENT OF EDUCATION AND SCIENCE (1980c) *Examinations 16–18*. London: HMSO.

DEPARTMENT OF EDUCATION AND SCIENCE (1981a) Circular 6/81 *The School Curriculum*. London: HMSO.

DEPARTMENT OF EDUCATION AND SCIENCE (1981b) *Curriculum 11–16: A Review of Progress*. London: HMSO.

DEPARTMENT OF EDUCATION AND SCIENCE (1981c) *The School Curriculum*. London: HMSO.

DEPARTMENT OF EDUCATION AND SCIENCE (1981d) *Review of the Schools Council*. London: HMSO.

DEPARTMENT OF EDUCATION AND SCIENCE (1982) *17 plus: A new qualification*. London: HMSO.

DEPARTMENT OF EDUCATION AND SCIENCE (1983a) Circular 8/83. *The School Curriculum*. London: HMSO.

DEPARTMENT OF EDUCATION AND SCIENCE (1983b) *Curriculum 11–16: Towards a Statement of Entitlement (Curricular Re-appraisal in Action)*. London: HMSO.

DEPARTMENT OF EDUCATION AND SCIENCE (1983c) *Records of Achievement at 16: some examples of current practice*. London: HMSO.

DEPARTMENT OF EDUCATION AND SCIENCE (1984) *Records of Achievement: A Statement of Policy*. London: HMSO.

DEPARTMENT OF EDUCATION AND SCIENCE (1985a) *Better Schools*. London: HMSO.

DEPARTMENT OF EDUCATION AND SCIENCE (1985b) *The Curriculum from 5 to 16* Curriculum Matters 2). London: HMSO.

DEPARTMENT OF EDUCATION AND SCIENCE (1986) *Local Authority Policies for the School Curriculum* (Report on the Circular 8/83 Review). London: HMSO.

DEPARTMENT OF EDUCATION AND SCIENCE AND WELSH OFFICE (1987a) *The National Curriculum 5–16: a consultation document*. London: HMSO.

DEPARTMENT OF EDUCATION AND SCIENCE (1987b) *Examination Reform for Schools: A Guide for Employers to Recent Changes in the School Examination and Assessment System.*

DEPARTMENT OF EDUCATION AND SCIENCE (1988a) *Report of the Committee of Inquiry into the Teaching of English Language* (Kingman Report). London: HMSO.

DEPARTMENT OF EDUCATION AND SCIENCE AND THE WELSH OFFICE (1988b) *National Curriculum: Task Group on Assessment and Testing: A Report.*

DEPARTMENT OF EDUCATION AND SCIENCE AND THE WELSH OFFICE (1988c) *National Curriculum: Three Supplementary Reports – Task Group on Assessment and Testing.*

DEPARTMENT OF EDUCATION AND SCIENCE AND THE WELSH OFFICE (1988d) *National Curriculum: Task Group on Assessment and Testing Report. A Digest for Schools.*

DEPARTMENT OF EDUCATION AND SCIENCE (1988e) *Advancing A Levels* (Higginson Report). Report of a Committee appointed by the Secretary of State for Education and Science and the Secretary of State for Wales. London: HMSO.

DWORKIN, R. (1977) *Taking Rights Seriously*. London: Duckworth.

ELIOT, T.S. (1948) *Notes Towards a Definition of Culture*. London: Faber.

GEERTZ, C. (1975) *The Interpretation of Culture*. New York: Basic Books.

GIPPS, C. (ed.) (1986) *The GCSE: an uncommon examination*. (Bedford Way Paper No. 29). London: Institute of Education University of London.

GEORGE, V. and WILDING, P. (1985) *Ideology and Social Welfare*. London: Routledge and Kegan Paul.

GULBENKIAN FOUNDATION (1982) *The Arts in Schools*. London: Calouste Gulbenkian Foundation.

HALSEY, A.H. (1983) 'Schools for Democracy' in AHIER, J. and FLUDE, M. (eds) *Contemporary Education Policy*. London: Croom Helm.

HIRST, P. (1975) *Knowledge and Curriculum*. London: Routledge and Kegan Paul.

HOLT, M. (1983) *Curriculum Workshop*. London: Routledge and Kegan Paul.

HOUSE OF COMMONS (1976) *Tenth Report from the Expenditure Committee Session 1975–76 Policy Making in the DES*. London: HMSO.

KING, E.J. (1979) *Other Schools and Ours*. New York: Holt, Reinehart and Winston.

KINGDON, M. and STOBART, G. (1988) *GCSE*. London: Falmer.

KLIEBARD, H.M. (1970) 'The Tyler Rationale' *School Review*, **78**, 259.

KLUCKHOHN, C. (1949) *Mirror for Man*. New York: Whittlesey House.

LAWTON, D. (1973) *Social Change, Educational Theory and Curriculum Planning*. London: University of London Press.

LAWTON, D. (1983) *Curriculum Studies and Educational Planning*. London: Hodder and Stoughton.

LAWTON, D. and GORDON, P. (1987) *HMI*. London: Routledge and Kegan Paul.

LAWTON, D. and CHITTY, C. (1988) *The National Curriculum*, (Bedford Way Paper 33). Institute of Education University of London.

LEE, D. (1960) 'Enduring Human Values' (mimeo) California Association for Nursery Education quoted by WESTBY-GIBSON, D. (1965) in *Social Perspectives on Education*. New York: Wiley.

LETWIN, O. (1988) *Privatising the World*. London:Cassell.

LEVI-STRAUSS, C. (1966) *The Savage Mind*. London: Heinemann.

LINTON, R. (ed.) (1940) *Acculturation*. New York: Appleton-Century-Crofts.

LODGE, D. (1978) *Changing Places*. London: Penguin.

MCPHAIL, P., UNGOED-THOMAS, J.R. and CHAPMAN, H. (1972) *Moral Education in the Secondary School*. Harlow: Longman.

MAGER, R.F. (1962) *Preparing Objectives for Programmed Instruction*. San Francisco, California, USA: Fearon.

MANZER, R.A. (1970) *Teachers and Politics*. Manchester: Manchester University Press.

MATHEWS, J.C. (1985) *Examinations*. London: Allen and Unwin.

MINISTRY OF EDUCATION (1959) (CACE) *15–18*. (Crowther Report). London: HMSO.

MINISTRY OF EDUCATION (Secondary School Examination Council) (1960) *Secondary School Examinations other than GCE* (Beloe Report). London: HMSO.

MOON, B. (1988) *Modular Curriculum*. London: Paul Chapman.

MORTIMORE, J., MORTIMORE, P. and CHITTY, C. (1986) *Secondary School Examinations. 'The Helpful Servants, not the dominating master'*. Bedford Way Papers 18. London: Institute of Education University of London.

NEILL, A.S. (1926) *The Problem Child*. London: Herbert Jenkins.

NUTTALL, D. (1986) 'What can we learn from research on teaching and appraisal?' in DOCKRELL, B., NISBET, J., NUTTALL, D., STONES, E. and WILCOX, B. *Appraising Appraisal*. Birmingham: British Educational Research Association (BERA).

PHENIX, P.H. (1964) *Realms of Meaning*. London: McGraw-Hill.

POPHAM, W.J. (1969) 'Objectives and Instruction' in POPHAM, W.J., EISNER, E.W., SULLIVAN, H.J. and TYLER, L.L. (eds) *Instructional Objectives*. Washington DC: AERA Monograph/ Rand McNally.

PRING, R. (1982) 'Personal and Social Development' *Cambridge Journal of Education*, **12**, 1, 3–1.

RAISON, T. (1976) *The Act and the Partnership*. London: Centre for Studies in Social Policy.

RAWLS, J.(1972) *A Theory of Justice*. London: Oxford University Press.

RODERICK, G. and STEVENS, M. (1981) *Where Did We Go Wrong? Industry, Education and Economy of Victorian England*. London: Falmer.

RODGER, I.A. and RICHARDSON, J.A.S. (1985) *Studies in Teaching and Learning: Self-evaluation for Primary Schools*, London: Hodder and Stoughton.

ROUSSEAU, JEAN-JACQUES (1762) *Emile* (various editions).

ROYAL COMMISSION ON SECONDARY EDUCATION (1895) (Bryce Report) PP. xliii– xlix.

SCHOOLS COUNCIL (1966) *Sixth-form Curriculum and Examinations*. Working Paper No.5. London: HMSO.

SCHOOLS COUNCIL (1975a) *Examinations at 16+: Proposal for the Future*. (Report of the Joint Examinations Sub-Committee of the Schools Council on a common system of examining at 16+ with an evaluation, conclusions and recommendations.) London: HMSO.

SCHOOLS COUNCIL (1975b) Working Paper 53 *The Whole Curriculum 13–16*. London: Evans/Methuen.

SCHOOLS COUNCIL (1975c) Working Paper 55 *The Curriculum in the Middle Years*. London: Evans/Methuen.

SCHOOLS COUNCIL (1979) *Comparability in Examinations*, Occasional Paper 1. Schools Council Forum on Comparability. London: Evans/Methuen.

SCHOOLS COUNCIL (1981) *The Practical Curriculum*. London: Methuen Educational.

SKILBECK, M. (1976) 'Ideologies and Values', Unit 3 of Course E203, *Curriculum Design and Development*: Milton Keynes: Open University.

SKILBECK, M. (1984) *School-Based Curriculum Development*. London: Harper and Row.

SKINNER, B.F. (1968) *The Technology of Teaching*. New York: Appleton-Century-Crofts.

STENHOUSE, L. (1970) 'Some Limitations of the Use of Objectives in Curriculum Research and Planning'. *Paedagogica Europaea*, **6**, 73–83.

TABA, H. (1962) *Curriculum Development*. New York: Harcourt, Brace and World.

TANNER, D. and TANNER, L. (1975) (revised edition 1980) *Curriculum Development*. London: Macmillan.

TAWNEY, R.H. (1926) *Religion and the Rise of Capitalism*. London: Penguin, 1938.

TAWNEY, R.H. (1931) *Equality*. London: Allen and Unwin, 1964.

THOMPSON, E.P. (1968) *The Making of the English Working Class*. Harmondsworth: Penguin.

TYLER, R.W. (1949) *Basic Principles of Curriculum and Instruction*. Chicago, Illinois: University of Chicago Press.

TYLER, R.W. (1973) 'The Father of Behavioural Objectives Criticises Them' *Phi Delta Kappan*, **55**, 57.

WARNOCK, M. (1988) *A Common Policy for Education*. London: Oxford University Press.

WEDELL, K. (1988) 'The National Curriculum and Special Educational Needs' in LAWTON, D. and CHITTY, C. (eds) *The National Curriculum*, Bedford Way Papers/33. Institute of Education, University of London.

WEINER, M.J. (1981) *English Culture and the Decline of the Industrial Spirit 1850–1980*. Cambridge: Cambridge University Press.

WHITE, J., BLACK, P., OGBORN, J., CRICK, B., PORTER, A., HORNSEY, A., ASPIN, D. and LAWTON, D. (1981) *No Minister: A Critique of the DES paper 'The School Curriculum'*. Bedford Way Paper 4. London: Institute of Education University of London.

Index

How does the school curriculum adjust to social change and to disciplines which impinge on the intellectual study of curriculum planning? What, in particular, are the forces underlying the advent of the National Curriculum in this country?

Using techniques of cultural analysis as a basis for curriculum planning, Professor Denis Lawton takes a broad look at the changes in education over the past fifty years. In particular, he concentrates on the educational and political events which have taken place since 1983, leading up to the implementation of the most significant legislation in education since 1944 – the 1988 Education Act – which he discusses in detail, both in the context of theories of education and social change and in the light of its implications for teachers.

Professor Denis Lawton is in a unique position as Director of the Institute of Education, University of London and as Chairman for the Consortium of Assessment and Testing in Schools, to offer a thoroughly informed book on this central issue at this time.

ISBN 0-340-50509-

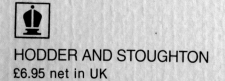

HODDER AND STOUGHTON
£6.95 net in UK

9 780340 505090

CHERWELL
VALLEY RAILWAY

THE SOCIAL HISTORY OF AN
OXFORDSHIRE RAILWAY

PETER ALLEN